FINDING MY VOICE

Finding My Voice

A
Young
Woman's
Perspective

Beth M. Knobbe

ST. ANTHONY MESSENGER PRESS
Cincinnati, Ohio

Humbly welcome the word that has been planted in you.
—James 1:21

Scripture passages have been taken from *New Revised Standard Version Bible,* copyright
©1989 by the Division of Christian Education of the National Council of the Churches of
Christ in the U.S.A., and used by permission. All rights reserved.

Book and cover design by Mark Sullivan
Cover image ©istockphoto.com/Carmen Martínez Banús

LIBRARY OF CONGRESS CATALOGING-IN-PUBLICATION DATA
Knobbe, Beth M.
Finding my voice : a young woman's perspective / Beth M. Knobbe.
p. cm. — (Called to holiness)
Includes bibliographical references (p.   ) and index.
ISBN 978-0-86716-894-5 (pbk. : alk. paper) 1. Young women—Religious life. 2.
Catholic women—Religious life. I. Title.
BX2347.8.Y66K66 2009
248.8'43—dc22
2009029058

ISBN 978-0-86716-894-5

Published by St. Anthony Messenger Press
28 W. Liberty St.
Cincinnati, OH 45202
www.SAMPBooks.org

www.CalledtoHoliness.org

Printed in the United States of America.

Printed on acid-free paper.

09 10 11 12 13 5 4 3 2 1

CONTENTS

ACKNOWLEDGMENTS

I owe a tremendous thank-you to Elizabeth Dreyer, general editor of the Called to Holiness series for her invitation and support in bringing this book to life. Her delicate balance of encouragement and critique, and her keen ability to gently call out my biases and blind spots have contributed to this book in ways that I could not have imagined.

My own journey toward "finding my voice" has included many people for whom I am especially grateful. I am grateful for the unwavering support of my family—Don, Dee, Becky, Jim, Curtis, Iva, Anna, Chet, Joseph and our entire extended family. I am blessed with an abundant community of friends, especially Abby Nall, Bridget Foley, Jenene Francis, JoEllen Cattapan, Lynn Stasior, Maureen Evers, Meredith McCarthy and various members of our women's prayer group. I am forever grateful to my fellow Amate House alumni for their loving support and faithful witness to the pursuit of justice. I also wish to thank the staff and students at the Sheil Catholic Center for their wisdom, inspiration and flexibility.

Each year, I am inspired by the people of Cusmapa, Nicaragua. I owe thanks to the Fabretto Children's Foundation, the many travel companions who have become friends on the journey, and to my brothers and sisters in Nicaragua who have taught me what it means to trust in God, love one's neighbor and live in solidarity with the rest of the world.

Finally, I am eternally grateful to Al Gustafson, who has spent countless hours teaching me how to listen for the voice of God deep within, to Father Ken Simpson who has been a wonderful mentor, to Father Tom Hurley for his poignant and prophetic words, and a sincere thanks to Susan Ross who provided the inspiration for the title of this book.

I wish to acknowledge the support and encouragement of an organization of philanthropists: Foundations and Donors Interested in Catholic Activities (FADICA). In January of 2005, I was invited to speak before this organization at a conference entitled Women of Faith. The discussion explored the many contributions of women to Roman Catholic ministry, church leadership and theology.

The members of FADICA heard my appeal for a renewed focus on women's spirituality in the context of significant religious change during the twentieth century and the pressing challenges of the twenty-first. The need for a creative, solidly grounded, and theologically sophisticated spirituality available in an accessible form for all Christian women seemed obvious. Follow-up conversations by the FADICA board, ably led by Frank Butler, led to a proposal from Fairfield University for a series of books on women's spirituality. Thus, FADICA, Fairfield University and St. Anthony Messenger Press formed a collaborative partnership to produce seven volumes under the title *Called to Holiness: Spirituality for Catholic Women.*

I wish to thank individuals and foundations whose generosity made this collaborative venture possible. These include the Amaturo Family Foundation, the AMS Fund, the Cushman Foundation, the Mary J. Donnelly Foundation, George and Marie Doty, Mrs. James Farley, the Robert and Maura Burke Morey Charitable Trust, Maureen O'Leary, Ann Marie Paine and the Raskob Foundation for Catholic Activities. I wish to extend a word of thanks and praise to the entire FADICA membership, whose conscientious, quiet and loving participation in shaping the life of the church has been an inspiration.

*The focus of this series is spirituality. Its interest is women of all back-*grounds: rich and poor; married and single; white, black and brown; gay and straight; those who are biological mothers and those who are mothers in other senses. There will be volumes on grassroots theology, family life, prayer, action for justice, grieving, young adult issues, wisdom years and Hispanic heritage. I hope all the volumes in this series will deepen and shape your own spiritual life in creative ways, as you engage with the theology of our rich, two-thousand-year-old Christian tradition.

Women's spiritualities are lived in light of their concrete, specific experiences of joy and struggle; ecstasy and despair; virtue and vice; work and leisure; family and friends; embodiment and sexuality; tears and laughter; sickness and health; sistering and mothering. These volumes are for women and men from all walks of life, whether they are new to the spiritual journey or old hands, affluent, middle-class or poor. Included in the circle we call church are persons from every country on the planet, some at the center, others at the margins or even beyond.

The time is ripe for "ordinary" women to be doing theology. The first and second waves of the women's movement in the nineteenth and twentieth centuries provided a valiant and solid foundation for the third wave which will mark, and be marked by, the world of the early twenty-first century. Changes and developments from one generation to the next makes our heads spin. Younger women readers are likely to be already grooming the soil for a fourth wave of Christian spirituality done by and for women. Women have always loved God, served others and struggled with sin, but the historical context has been less than friendly in terms of women's dignity, acknowledgment of female gifts and empowerment by church and society. In a time of growing emphasis on the role of clergy, and the backlash against women in society, the voices of the laity—especially the voices of women—are needed more than ever.

The Greek language has two words for time. *Chronos* points to the time signaled by the hands on the clock—for example, it is a quarter past two. *Kairos* points to time that is ripe, a moment pregnant with possibility. As Christian women, we live in a time rightly described as *kairos*. It is a time that calls us, demands of us renewed energy, reflection and commitment to attend to and help each other grow spiritually as we seek to love ourselves and the world. At this point in history, the fruit of women's struggle includes new self-awareness, self-confidence and self-respect. More and more women are beginning to see just how lovable and capable they are. The goal of the Christian life has always been to lay down our lives in love for the other, but the particular ways this vocation is lived out differ from era to era and place to place. Women's ability to voice with confidence the phrase, "I am a theologian" at the beginning of the twenty-first century means something it could not have meant even fifty years ago.

Those who were part of the early waves of feminism celebrate the hard-won accomplishments of the women's movement and know that this work needs to be taken up by future generations. Young women in their twenties and thirties are often unaware of past efforts that brought about more dignity and freedom for women. Women have opened many doors, but many remain closed. The media have recently explored the plight of Hindu widows in India; less publicized is that women in the United States still earn only seventy-seven cents for every dollar earned by their male counterparts. We must be vigilant and continue to act for decades to come in order to secure our accomplishments thus far and make further inroads toward the creation of a just, egalitarian world. Those who sense that the women's movement is in a doldrums inspire us to renew the enthusiasm and dedication of our foremothers.

When we cast our eye beyond the women of our own nation, it takes but a split-second to realize that the majority of the world's poor and oppressed are women. A quick visit to the Women's Human Rights Watch Web site reveals the breadth and depth of women's oppression across the globe from poverty and domestic abuse to sex slavery. Most women (and their children) do not have enough to eat, a warm, dry place to sleep or access to education. Female babies are more at risk than male babies. Women, more than men, lack the protection of the law and the respect of their communities. The double-standard in sexual matters affects women in harmful ways in all cultures and economic groups across the globe.

For all of these reasons it is not just important—but pressing, crucial, urgent—that all women of faith own the title "theologian" and shape this role in light of each woman's unique set of characteristics, context, relationships and spiritualities. We are theologians when we sort through our experience and the great and small problems of our time through reflection on Scripture or the words of a mystic or theologian. The images of God that emerged for Paul, Augustine or Catherine of Siena provide guidance, but their theology cannot ever be a substitute for our own. Theology helps us shape what we think about God, justice, love, the destiny of humanity and the entire universe in a way that is relevant to the specific issues facing us in the twenty-first century. The call to spiritual depths and mystical heights has never been more resounding.

Elizabeth A. Dreyer
Series Editor

• THE VOICE THAT ECHOES •

"I think you would make a wonderful eco-theologian!" There is a lot of truth in that statement for any young woman reading this book. I'm guessing that you've never heard of an eco-theologian. Until a few years ago, I had never heard the term either and it wasn't until I started writing this book that I really began to consider the meaning of that statement.

During the summer of 2003, I spent twelve days volunteering in the remote village of San Jose de Cusmapa, Nicaragua. This annual trip is part of a global outreach program sponsored by Old St. Patrick Church in Chicago where I've been a member for many years. Additional trips are now hosted by the Sheil Catholic Center at Northwestern University where I serve as campus minister. We spent our days playing games with the kids in the after-school program and planting trees in the local pine forest. With no TV, no radio and no Internet service, our evenings were marked by conversation, card games and storytelling. Midway through the trip, someone posed this question, "If you could leave your job tomorrow and spend the rest of your life doing what you love, what would you do?"

At the time, I was a consultant and project manager working on pension plan administration. Several people commented on how much I love spending time outdoors, and how I seem so comfortable leading morning prayer. I was humored by the group's suggestions that I might make a good teacher, missionary or retreat master. Our church's director of adult faith formation then made an observation about the hours I spent gazing at the sunset and my intuitive sense of God's presence among the people living in this poor village. "I think you would make a wonderful eco-theologian!" he said. I laughed. I had never heard of an eco-theologian, yet I smiled and nodded in agreement as if I completely understood. Later that night, I pulled out my journal and wrote down the word *echo-theologian*. It wasn't until the following day, as I pondered Terry's comments about nature that I realized he meant *eco* (as in ecology) and not *echo* (as in the reverberating sound one hears when speaking into a deep canyon).

Terry was not completely off the mark. Five years later, having completed a master of divinity degree and four subsequent trips to Nicaragua, that first experience continues to have a profound impact on my life. I occasionally dream about becoming an eco-theologian (focusing on the relationship between spirituality and the environment), but I am fascinated at the prospect of doing "echo"-theology.

Like the sound of an echo that vibrates through the air, the voice of God speaks in a way that echoes in our souls. There are profound moments that make a ripple effect on our lives, experiences that shake us to the core and stories we tell over and over again in an attempt to better understand their meaning and significance. "Echo"-theology holds open the possibility that God will shout a divine word into the hollow void, and that that word will reverberate as far as it can until it settles into an open space within our souls.

The prophet Isaiah reminds us that divine words roam the world with a life of their own and are restless until they have effected change.

> For as the rain and the snow come down from heaven,
>   and do not return there until they have watered the earth,
>   making it bring forth and sprout,
>   giving seed to the sower and bread to the eater,
>   so shall my word be that goes out from my mouth;
>   it shall not return to me empty,
>   but it shall accomplish that which I purpose,
>   and succeed in the thing for which I sent it. (Isaiah 55:10–11)

When the voice of God speaks, it reverberates with grace. Ordinary moments in life that delight and surprise us leave a hint of God's presence. Tragedy and disaster are filled with God's invitation to become voices of peace and agents of change. The voice of God echoes when we encounter beauty, when hospitality is extended, when we fall in love or fall to our knees in prayer. Moments of grace, those reminders of God's constant presence and unfailing care, are God's echo in the world.

The young adult years are filled with unforgettable moments—moments that resound with meaning. It is a time in life when women make decisions that guide and direct their futures. Recent high school and college graduates look forward to new opportunities. Young professionals steep themselves in career aspirations. Newly married couples stand on the threshold of a lifetime of dreams. And many young adults enjoy the freedom that comes with the single years. The young adult years are a time to listen, and a time to discern among the many voices that inspire, encourage, advise and invite. It is a time to discover the voice that whispers deep within.

Finding My Voice

This book is intended for young adult women seeking to discover their voice. It is for sisters, girlfriends and students. It is for the girl next door on her way out to spend a Saturday night with friends, and for the group of young moms gathered at the local coffee shop with strollers in tow. It is for women finding their way in the world—married and single, lesbian and straight, those with children and those without.

I hope this book will be a helpful and insightful resource for men and women, lay and ordained, who work with young adults—as well as parents and grandparents who also want to understand the distinctive needs and challenges of today's young women. It is for teachers, professors, pastors, campus ministers, spiritual directors and anyone who finds themselves counseling, consoling or befriending women in their twenties and thirties.

Most especially, this book was written for any woman hoping to find her voice amid the myriad of well-meaning, idealistic, critical, supportive and challenging voices in our society today. I hope that spiritual seekers and lifelong Catholics will hear their stories echoed in these pages. It is for all women who seek to do theology, especially this kind of grassroots theology that works to make sense of God's action in the world and in our lives. We "do theology" when we take our life experience and bounce it off the wisdom of the church. As we listen and examine our own stories, we discover the way our stories ripple through Scripture, and we hear the stories of our lives echoed in the lives of saints.

"Echo"-theology is about noticing the deep reverberations of life. It is for anyone who desires to listen intently for the voice of God through the exciting and ever-changing experiences of falling in love, starting a career, maintaining friendships, discovering hidden talents and enduring the up-and-down moments of everyday life. As we listen intently, we begin to know God's voice in prayer, in our work, in our relationships and in our response to the needs of the world. Our very lives become God's echo as we attend to the breath of life, the cry for justice and the whisper of the Spirit's wisdom. *Finding My Voice* is about discovering the true voice that resonates deep within and knowing it as an echo of the voice of God.

CHAPTER ONE

• SPIRITUALITY FOR GENERATION X AND Y (WHY?) •

…be patient toward all that is unsolved in your heart and try to love the *questions themselves.…* Do not now seek the answers, which cannot be given you because you would not be able to live them. And the point is, to live everything. *Live* the questions now. Perhaps you will then gradually, without noticing it, live along some distant day into the answer.

—Ranier Maria Rilke, *Letters to a Young Poet*[1]

Ask and it will be given to you; search and you will find; knock, and the door will be opened for you. For everyone who asks receives; and everyone who searches finds, and for everyone who knocks, the door will be opened.

—Matthew 7:7–8

"Can I ask you a question?" I get this request often—in all its various forms:
   "Do you have time for a question?"
   "Can I ask you something?"
   "What do you think about this?"
   "Can we talk?"
   I always respond in the affirmative, although with a bit of hesitation. I'm never really certain what the person standing in front of me is about

to ask. It's not that I'm frightened by the questions; I'm just fairly certain that I don't have all the answers to questions like: *Why is life unfair? Should I be dating this person? How do I know if he's the right one? I'm thinking about quitting school: Is that a good idea or not? What if I don't want to be a doctor? Do you think I should tell my parents? Can you explain the nature of the Trinity? How do I know if God hears my prayers?*

As a campus minister, I get questions that range from finding the perfect boyfriend to choosing a career path to looking for new ways to pray. At times, they are philosophical questions about human existence and our relationship with God. And every so often, I get questions about church doctrine or about a life of service in the church.

I've come to realize that asking provocative questions is at the heart of the young adult experience. Those in their twenties and thirties ask questions because they are confronted with certain situations for the first time. They suddenly find themselves seeking answers to questions that were not important until now. As young adults grow into a sense of independence and self awareness, the questions become more profound and more numerous than the answers.

Important questions invite complex answers. Today's seekers face many of the same questions as previous generations. They wonder about their relationships, careers and finding meaning in life, but these questions are asked in new ways. Those growing up in the United States are asking these questions through the lens of a well-educated population, living in a diverse and pluralistic society, and from a generation completely reliant on technology. We want answers, and we want them now.

Like those before them, members of the Millennial generation (born 1982–2002)[2] seek to understand the world in which they live, and they have a deep desire to know their place within it. Also known as Generation Y (or Generation Why?), they are a contemporary age group defined by their quest for creative solutions. Technology has equipped them with Google, Yahoo! and Wikipedia. These tools have only increased their curiosity for knowledge and understanding, while historic events of their time—natural disasters, a shifting economy and concerns about global security—often bring more uncertainty than assurance.

The wisdom of Rilke to "live the questions" in order to "live into the answers" requires patience, dealing with uncertainty and living with ambiguity. On the surface, there is an apparent contradiction between Rilke's insight, "Do not seek the answers, which cannot be given" and Matthew's testimony, "For everyone who asks, receives; and everyone who searches finds." Should we ask or remain silent? Should we seek or refrain from searching? It is not easy to remain silent in the face of ambiguity or to do nothing while waiting for clarity. Both Matthew and Rilke invite us to trust in something bigger than ourselves. God knows our needs, hears our questions and understands our plea for answers. God wants to give us everything we need to help us through these maturing years. The answers to our questions will come, and they will be given in due time. Our soul searching requires asking *and* waiting; seeking *and* being still. We ask profound questions with openness and generosity of heart—attentive to the moment, prepared to welcome and ready to receive those things which God knows are good for us.

Wisdom is what we derive from reflecting on our experience, learning how the world works and responding to it. We do not always find the answers as soon as we would like nor do we always receive the answers we want to hear. While there is a lot of information available on the World Wide Web, answers to life's deepest questions cannot be found online, even with the most sophisticated search engine.

Are We There Yet?

We all remember the proverbial question asked by every little kid during a long car trip, "Are we there yet?" Many of us remember the excitement and anxiety of a long car ride, the endless waiting and the occasional whining that accompanied a trip to Grandma's house, a much-anticipated vacation spot or the final stretch as we headed toward the comfort of home. Interestingly, this same question recently surfaced during a weekend retreat with college students. "Are we *there* yet?!" Only "there" was not some favorite destination. Rather, "there" referred to the things we look forward to, but have not yet achieved. For this group of young people, the question specifically pertained to the journey of growing up and becoming an adult. When does someone arrive at adulthood? How do I know that I'm *there*?

Previous generations marked adulthood by marriage, home ownership, financial independence, having children and career advancement. Today, the age gap between adolescence and adulthood grows ever wider. While we celebrate certain milestones on the way to adulthood (sixteen to drive, eighteen to vote, twenty-one to purchase alcohol), there is no magical age when one becomes a grown-up. Furthermore, today's young adults are taking more time to achieve the traditional milestones, which is something that makes our parents, grandparents and older siblings a bit nervous.

Those in their twenties and thirties comprise the last remaining years of Generation X (those born between 1961–1981) and of the Millennial generation. They are getting married later; they are more likely to make multiple moves before settling in a geographical location; they change jobs more frequently; and spend more time in and out of relationships. In recent years, more and more young adults are moving home after college. Perhaps this is a reflection of the fluctuating economy, a hypercompetitive job market or the "helicopter syndrome" of parents who hover over their child's every move well beyond adolescence. While young adults are often perceived as "delaying" adulthood, this is certainly not their intention.

Young people are not waiting on tomorrow to fulfill their dreams; they are living very full and productive lives. An entry-level job, a year spent traveling, studying abroad or volunteering for a nonprofit organization is not wasted time. It is time spent in self-discovery, learning about the world and gaining valuable experience. I often hear young adults say that being single is more than just waiting to get married. Women and men have discovered that they can start a career, buy a home, plan the perfect vacation and develop personal interests without a permanent partner. This in-between time is itself becoming a phase of life.

The other hallmark of this generation is that we live in a culture of immediacy. With the onslaught of technology, we expect to have everything now. We've become accustomed to having instant results and information at our fingertips. Virtual communication tools—laptop, cell phone, pager, Blackberry—provide us with the means to stay connected and to be available 24/7 if we choose. Technology has conditioned us to live in the moment. Social networking sites (like MySpace, Facebook and Twitter) and endless personal blog entries focus on what people are doing right *now*. We expect an up-to-the-minute status on our friends' lives, while live newscasts from around the world make yesterday's news old news. Life quickly changes from one moment to the next. Millennials value flexibility. They are adept at multitasking and quickly adapt to change.

Living from one moment to the next seems perfectly natural to those growing up in the computer age. If there is any guarantee in life today, it is that things will change. Computers are practically out of date and in need of an upgrade not long after you take them out of the box! Likewise, if we are unsatisfied with a job, bored with where we live or unhappy in a relationship then surely there is another one waiting not far down the road. With lives constantly in flux, it is no surprise that the traditional rites of passage, often marked by their permanence, have begun to shift.

For most young adults, delaying traditional adulthood is not intentional. It's not that we are not concerned with getting married, settling into a home or establishing a career. Believe me; nothing is more disconcerting to a single woman in her late twenties than being met with comments from well-meaning friends and family members who don't understand why she is not married. Change is inevitable when we live in a culture that is constantly on the go. It affects every facet of our lives, and the cultural influences often seem far beyond our control.

A high-tech, on-demand, fast-paced culture presents a lot of questions for spiritual seekers. Are we energized by constant change or does it wear us out? How do we respond to the "in-between" phase? Are we in a hurry to get through it? Do we ignore it or try to occupy our time with other things? It sometimes feels like the road to adulthood cannot move fast enough. In a fast-paced world, there is an underlying assumption that our dreams will somehow pass us by if we don't get to them now. We are impatient to be on the way.

I am reminded of the light-hearted aphorism: "Patience is a virtue; possess it as you can; Found often in a woman; and rarely in a man!" Patience becomes an important virtue in the age of speed. And yet, our fast-paced world has not prepared us well or given us tools for waiting. It seems that we are always in a hurry, looking forward to the next big moment. We deal with discontent by doing something about it. Entire industries are designed around calendars, day planners and organizational tools. But when do these tools turn into yet another pressure to plan and meet deadlines? We are always looking forward to the next big event—whether that means making plans for Saturday night or counting the days until summer vacation.

What might we find if we slow down? Are we able to consciously live in the moment aware of all that it contains? How much do we really know about ourselves? What value is there in waiting? Waiting is an active, not a passive activity. Our waiting is not a matter of not doing anything. Rather, we wait and trust that something good is happening. The "in-between" phase is a hopeful time. It holds the promise that new opportunities are on the horizon, and good things do come to those who wait. The profound things of God cannot be rushed.

Once a year, usually in the dead of winter, my friends get together for a night of chili and board games. Robert's secret recipe includes letting the chili simmer for an entire day—overnight, if possible. He insists on allowing time to let the spices soak in. It is a process that cannot be hurried. Turning up the heat only increases the temperature. Adding more seasoning overpowers the flavor. The perfect pot of chili requires using the right amount of spice and allowing the flavors to unfold and intensify with time. There is a subtle temptation to turn up the heat, to stick it in the microwave, or to fast forward through the process. Likewise, we cannot microwave faith. The spiritual journey is one that needs to simmer and deliberately wait for the soul to unfold. Spiritual writer Sue Monk Kidd says of our impatience, "It's as if we imagine that all of our spiritual growth potential is dehydrated contents to which we need only add some holy water to make it instantly and easily appear."[3]

The spiritual life is a life in which we wait. I imagine our lives unfold as if God is cooking a large pot of soup. God has creatively combined the right people, places and experiences, actively attentive to the ways they intersect and complement one another. We trust that something is happening, even if we cannot see it. We wait in hope, confident that something good has been started, and it will be brought to completion in God's time.

Are we there yet? It is an important question for a generation that is constantly changing, plugged in and always on the go. To find the answer, we will have to wait.

How Much Is Enough? Living in a Consumer-Driven Culture

Not long ago, Megan, a recent college graduate, described the politics of her office and the cavernous divide between herself and colleagues who were old enough to be her parents. It is no surprise that this twenty-something single woman has different social expectations, spending habits, interests outside of work and is a bit more tech-savvy than her more experienced coworkers. But her greatest frustration was, "I've not earned the right to speak."

It is the classic catch-22 for any young adult seeking to get ahead in a career. Employers are looking for people with experience, and you cannot gain any experience unless you find someone willing to take a chance on someone with no experience. Megan was looking for a place where her suggestions, creativity, hard work and dedication would be sought and appreciated, but her inexperience seemed to be holding her back. In this first year out of college, she was learning the delicate balance of when to speak up and when to listen; when to push forward and when to stay silent; when to rely on the wisdom of coworkers and when to take a risk—knowing that she would either learn from her mistakes or reap her rewards.

Women have forged paths at a great cost, making space for our generation. It was not all that long ago when women were expected to be seen and not heard. While the gender gap still exists in many professions, women *are* making their voices heard. Young girls are told that they can be whatever they want to be and, for the most part, this is true. Long gone are the days when women were limited to professional careers as teachers, nurses, nuns and stay-at-home moms.

The first wave of feminism in the United States focused on the women's suffrage movement of the late nineteenth and early twentieth century. Women campaigned for the abolition of slavery and successfully lobbied for the passage of the Nineteenth Amendment, which granted women the right to vote. Later feminist movements focused on social and cultural inequalities—advocating on behalf of women in the workplace, women's role in politics and equal representation in government. They also brought attention to important issues such as gender-based discrimination and sexual harassment.

Our moms and aunts were the first to crack the glass ceiling, and today young women continue to push open the skylight. Women have slowly inched their way into professions traditionally dominated by men. Recent statistics show that women represent 47 percent of all law school attendees, 48 percent of the medical school population and 35 percent of seminary enrollment.[4] Women have every reason to be proud of their accomplishments and grateful to those who have helped pave the way.

Yet, women still struggle to be recognized for their ideas, contributions and to receive equal pay; but in other ways the pendulum has swung the other direction. We've gone from not having the same opportunities as men to an expectation that you can, and should, do it all. You can be anything you want to be. You can have anything you want. (And you *should*.) Success is defined by having it "all"—career, family, mortgage, marriage, the list goes on. At the same time, some women really agonize over whether to pursue an advanced degree, stay at home to raise a family or enter a profession. Meanwhile, most men do not seem to share this angst, and work-life balance is not a concern until marriage and family become a reality.

We live in a consumer-driven culture where success is often defined by getting ahead and measured by the amount of material goods we own. Ours is a society that places a higher value on things that cost more—from cars to clothes to condos. Consumerism creates an unnecessary and unhealthy sense of competition. When our possessions become status symbols, we risk basing our self-worth on our material possessions rather than on the values we embody and embrace. Growing up in a privileged culture creates a sense of entitlement—not only do I want good things for my life, but I *deserve* them, society *owes* me. I will go to any length to get them and will become angry and resentful if I don't. Don't we all know a "bridezilla"? Women, selfish to the extreme, who go to outrageous lengths to plan the perfect wedding, as if it is all about *her* and *her* special day? I had a student who worked one summer in a bridal consultant firm. She said she was often nauseated all day at the arrogance, selfishness and egoism of brides she served. In another arena, a friend of mine was recently deploring the unrealistic expectations of a newly hired employee—a recent college graduate unhappy with the standard salary adjustment and devastated that she wasn't promoted to management level within the first six months on the job.

Setting goals and having high aspirations in life and even a healthy sense of competition are not bad things. But having outrageous expectations or defining success as having it *all*, can leave young adults with a lot of insecurity and questions: How much is enough? What does it mean to be successful? How do I know when I've made it? How do I balance the pressure to build a successful career and the desire to raise a family? Can I do it all and still stay true to myself?

Have you ever met someone who is trying too hard to be someone they're not? They come across as awkward, uncomfortable, phony or fake. On the other hand, have you ever noticed how beautiful a woman is when she is being herself? There is something very attractive about people who are comfortable in their own skin. We all know people who are authentic—famous or not-so-famous people who are truly genuine and down-to-earth folks. They're confident without being pompous; proud of their accomplishments without being conceited; perhaps wealthy but not pretentious. I think about Mother Teresa, Princess Diana, skating champion Michelle Kwan and First Lady Michelle Obama. I find myself intrigued and somewhat envious of them. Authentic people are genuinely beautiful people.

Being yourself is the best person you can be. It is easy to get caught up with the latest fads and fashions, lost in the crowd and worried about others' perceptions. Are we quick to follow what everyone else is doing without thinking it through for ourselves? In a young adult culture that values a frenzied lifestyle, one of the greatest challenges is staying grounded and remaining true to oneself. Truly having it all is to become your whole self and be authentically you.

Are You Saved?

Faith presents a big question mark for many young adults. Religion does not always fit comfortably within our culture. Attitudes about faith range from highly skeptical to mildly curious to fully committed.

Some of the most important catchwords for this generation include openness, acceptance, tolerance and diversity. Young adults growing up in a secular society are taught to be respectful of those who hold different religious perspectives, so as not to offend or exclude another person based on their belief system.

However, recently I had an encounter with my downstairs neighbor, Sean, at our mailboxes. We began talking about the Christmas wreath on the front door of our apartment building which was hung by the girl who lives across the hall. I made a casual comment about how nice it was to see people spreading holiday cheer, when Sean sarcastically remarked, "She must be one of those happy-go-lucky Christian-types." His comment seemed somewhat odd, as there was nothing overtly religious about the wreath. Noticing my puzzled look, he quickly apologized and said, "Oh, are you Christian?"

I replied, "Yes, as a matter of fact, I am. Are you?"

And he said, "Oh, no, I'm not Christian. I'm Catholic."

I always laugh half-heartedly when I tell that story. I wonder if Sean's comment is representative of some young adults (Catholic and Protestant) who know little about their faith and its relation to the larger Christian world. Perhaps Sean's reluctance to identify himself as "Christian" was a reference to those Christians who are not ashamed to wear their faith on their sleeve—or in the case of our neighbor—to display it on their front door. Or maybe his response was a way to disassociate himself from Christians who engage in aggressive proselytizing, or the self-righteous voices and behaviors of some politically driven Christians who tend to turn off even the most tolerant people.

What does it mean to be Catholic? It is an important question for young adults immersed in a pluralistic culture. For some, being Catholic might include going to Mass on Sunday, celebrating the sacraments, serving the poor, or adhering to a set of moral principles. This question is especially important for a generation that is not steeped in Catholic culture like our parents and grandparents were. Catholic identity can be fluid and tenuous, even for those of us who grew up going to Mass every week. My grandparents lived in a world in which every kid on the block was Catholic and all attended the same neighborhood parish and Catholic school. Younger Catholics are more likely to have neighbors, friends, classmates and coworkers who are Methodists, Jews, Muslims and atheists. The boundaries and markers of Catholicism are wide and varied given the time and circumstances in which we live.

Today's young adults are the first generation to grow up entirely in the post–Second Vatican Council period. Some of us were raised by parents and grandparents who yearn for the great church traditions of Catholicism—fasting from meat on Friday, women with heads covered in church, praying novenas and singing Latin hymns. On the other hand, many attended schools and parishes that enthusiastically embraced the expanded role of the laity, guitar Masses and canned food drives. I imagine that most of us find ourselves somewhere in between, with an assortment of spiritual, social and cultural traditions. While my earliest memories of the church include Mother of Perpetual Help devotions and memorizing answers from the *Baltimore Catechism*, I also spent a fair amount of time singing Christmas carols at the nursing home and attending World Youth Day celebrations.

Young adults are incredibly diverse in their practice of Catholicism. There are those who embrace time-honored devotional practices such as the rosary and Eucharistic Adoration. Other young people feel a strong connection to the church's social mission and outreach to the poor and marginalized. Still others are inspired by the praise-and-worship style of music adopted from mainstream Evangelical churches. And there are many who identify themselves as culturally Catholic— perhaps maintaining some spiritual practices on their own, but limiting their Mass attendance to Christmas, Easter, weddings and funerals.

Finally, let's not forget that the United States has a long history of being an immigrant homeland. The Catholic church in America reflects a great diversity of ethnic influences, and local church communities might include traditions that reflect their Native American, Hispanic, Asian or European roots. Filipino communities celebrate *Simbang Gabi*, a nine-day series of Masses held in preparation for Christmas. Mexican households construct altars to honor their beloved deceased for *Dia de los Muertos* (Day of the Dead or All Soul's Day). Italian families might set a Saint Joseph's table, while Czech families observe devotions to the Infant of Prague. In a country as diverse as the United States, many of our Catholic traditions reflect both our religious identity and our cultural heritage.

Spiritual But Not Religious

One phrase that has captured the imagination of this generation is: "I am *spiritual* but not religious." What does this mean? A quick survey offers a glimpse at what young adults mean when they use this phrase to describe themselves or their friends:

> I will readily admit that I don't think about spirituality and religion that often. Spirituality has had a simple meaning in my mind, believing in a being that does not take a form on this earth. Religion is a celebration of that belief. When I hear people describe themselves as "spiritual but not religious," I usually take it to mean that they believe in a higher power of some kind but have chosen not to partake in any sort of ritual recognizing and celebrating that higher power. —*Erica, 25*

> I've talked to many young Catholics who feel alienated from the church, and they don't particularly care for the "religious" part of being Catholic (going to Mass regularly and celebrating the sacraments). I think this is because they often do not know that any other way exists in the church. However, these same people say they are very spiritual. They still believe in God and Jesus but not the institution of the Catholic church. They believe deeply that something transcends them and their human selves. —*Bridget, 22*

13

In our consumer culture where you can pick from one of twenty toothpaste brands, I think some people have a tendency to want to shop around for a belief system. I suspect that when someone says they are "spiritual but not religious" they feel they have not yet bought into one of the prepackaged belief systems offered by mainstream traditions and churches. —*Anne, 29*

Some critics suggest that claiming to be "spiritual but not religious" is a polite way of backing down from the demands of maintaining a religious affiliation, and their concerns are not unwarranted. There are young adults who hide behind feel-good spirituality, seeking only those experiences which bring about a heightened sense of God's presence. In an era of self-help books, many people fall into the trap of do-it-yourself spirituality and concede, "I don't need the church to tell me how to live my life." Our culture of independence and individualism supports the notion that spirituality is something "just between me and God." In our consumer society, we tend to treat Mass like a concert or a corporate training course where people can say, "I stopped going to Mass because I wasn't getting anything out of it." More attractive Sunday activities include playing in a sports league, sleeping in or shopping. Somehow church just doesn't fit into our schedules.

On the other hand, there are many young adults for whom spirituality plays a genuinely important role, and their hesitations about the institutional church are worth paying attention to. Some are angered by a perceived hypocrisy in the church. Others have been hurt by the actions or unresponsiveness of a community or an individual. A single interaction can leave a sour taste for a long time. A young mom with a fussy child is told that it would be better for everyone if she stood in the back or waited outside. A bride and groom are forced to jump through hoops during their wedding preparations because one of them is not Catholic. I distinctly remember an unpleasant experience with the sacrament of reconciliation. Even after making an honest confession, I was sorely reprimanded and wondered if my sins were really forgiven.

Women in particular continue to be alienated from a male-dominated church—when the church has been slow to invite women as altar servers, lectors, ministers of the Eucharist, catechists and in various leadership roles at a local or global level. For generations, women have asked important questions about the church's teaching on sexuality, birth control, divorce, annulment and women's ordination. It is sometimes easier to adopt a "spiritual but not religious" stance, when our questions are dismissed or our stories go untold. What often makes the news about the church is financial misconduct or sexual abuse. This new generation continues to ask, what is the Good News when all we hear about is the bad news of the church?

Finally, there are those whose circumstances (death, divorce, families who frequently moved and interreligious marriage) prevented them from establishing roots in a community of faith, or who were dealt an unfair hand at an early age. I know a woman whose mom died when she was twelve years old and another whose parents got divorced when she was fifteen. Both of them stopped going to church during their college years. One woman admits that she was angry at God for a long time. It wasn't until her early thirties, when she was married and had children of her own, that she was ready to give the church another try.

Religion and spirituality are not separate entities. On the contrary, religion and spirituality are integrally linked. Spirituality is more than achieving stillness of mind, quietness of heart or a balanced life. Religion is more than blind acceptance of doctrine or rigid adherence to rules. Religious practices give voice to spirituality, and spirituality gives meaning to our rites and rituals. Spirituality without religion is empty belief, and religion without spirituality is uninspiring.

In the opening volume of this series, *Making Sense of God*, Elizabeth Dreyer makes a wonderful distinction between spirituality and theology:

> Spirituality is the journey of falling in love with God and living
> out that love in everyday life. It might include service to the poor,
> support of causes that contribute to the common good, spiritual

practices, developing a life of virtue. Theology is ordered reflection, in which we interrogate our experiences in order to name and make sense of them from a faith perspective. Where is God in this? Who is the God lurking behind our attitudes, behaviors and prayer? Who are we in the sight of God?[5]

To be both spiritual and religious is to recognize that all of life exists in relationship to God. Instead of compartmentalizing our life, we see all of life as one contiguous plane where our work, personal relationships, family and social activities are not separate but essential to the spiritual life. Every situation presents an opportunity for God's grace to enter into the conversation. It happens when a friend moves or a parent dies; when a spouse goes off to war or when families face tough economic times; when a young woman is faced with an unexpected pregnancy or a newly married couple grieves a miscarriage. Our relationship with God is not separate from the world. Our hopes and dreams for the future become the seedbed for discernment. Our ethical questions play host to wisdom of the Catholic tradition. Every disappointment and doubt carries with it the hope and promise of resurrection. The mystery of the Incarnation reminds us that God is intimately involved with the world. God wants to be in this messy, murky, beautiful, mysterious and grace-filled adventure with us.

Ask Provocative Questions

So, where does this leave the searching, seeking and sometimes "spiritual but not religious" young adults of today? I'd like to propose a patron saint for spiritual seekers—the Samaritan woman who meets Jesus at Jacob's well (John 4:1–42). Like many women in Scripture, we don't know her name, and she only appears in this one place in John's Gospel. In her anonymity, she could be any one of us. I imagine that she may have felt alienated from her Jewish roots, in the same way that some young adults feel alienated from the church. Like today's spiritual seekers, she is often misunderstood and easily dismissed as unfaithful.

Samaria (a region in central Israel) was inhabited by the Jewish people, until it was conquered by the Assyrians in 722 BC. Many of the Jews were exiled, and those who stayed were ostracized by the Jewish community because they intermarried with the Assyrians. Jewish travelers purposely avoided Samaria, and those traveling from Judea (in the south) to Galilee (in the north) frequently took a circuitous route. The very fact that Jesus went through Samaria, let alone that he stopped in Sychar, was surprising. Furthermore, it was highly unusual to see a man speaking with a woman in public, as women were not permitted to speak to unrelated men outside the home.

Through their conversation, Jesus is constantly drawing this woman into relationship. They banter about the fact that he does not have a bucket and how he will retrieve the living water which he promises. "Are you greater than our father Jacob who gave us the well?" she asks (John 4:12). Jesus explains that *he* is the source of this eternal water. She is intrigued, "Sir, give me this water, so that I may not be thirsty or have to keep coming here to draw water" (John 4:15). As she becomes more inquisitive, the questions become more personal. Jesus asks her to call her husband, revealing the most intimate details of her life, "for you have had five husbands, and the one you have now is not your husband" (John 4:18). Moving from one sensitive subject to another, she pushes back with a question about the appropriate place of worship. Jesus foretells a day "when true worshipers will worship the Father in spirit and truth" (John 4:23). She has already suspected he is a prophet, and now he has revealed something to her that few people understand. He is the one who will restore true worship to all of Israel. A whole new level of trust is generated with this question. He knows intimate details about her life; and now she knows something deeply personal about him.

At the end of their conversation, she says that she knows the Messiah is coming and "when he comes, he will tell us everything" (John 4:25). It is then that Jesus identifies himself as the Messiah. "I am he, the one who is speaking to you" (John 4:26). She drops everything to go tell the rest of the village about him. The people of the town come to him and are equally captivated, so much so that they invite him to stay for two more days. This woman is the first person to whom Jesus identifies himself as the Messiah, and it is because of her testimony that the people of Samaria begin to believe in him.

We often miss this dramatic point, because we get caught in the details of their conversation. Some scholars interpret the initial scene at the well as a woman of the night coming to gather water during the day in order to avoid being seen by other women of the village. They portray her as an outcast, even among the other women of the village. We are told that the woman has five husbands, and some immediately assume that "having five husbands" means that she is sleeping around.

In fact, there is nothing in the text or ancient world to explain why she came at noon, and nothing to support the (mis)perception that she was a prostitute or avoiding other women. We assume she was embarrassed about her situation and avoiding the other women, but we rarely question why she was going back to the well in the middle of the day. Could she have simply needed to fetch more water? Perhaps she had an unusually large quantity of laundry, unexpected company or extra cleaning that day?

Contemporary scholars also suggest John is using a play on words. The word for husband, *baal*, is also a word used to describe false gods. Given John's frequent use of irony and metaphor, the entire story could be read as an analogy for the sins of Israel and the false gods of the Samaritan people.

Jesus is never presented as disapproving of the women he encounters, and he does not hesitate to speak with them. Her gender is not a barrier to her belief or her abilities as a witness to this encounter with Christ. Regardless of her marital situation and how it is viewed by the community, she is able to speak articulately and has the necessary theological knowledge to engage in complex conversation with Jesus. Her unfortunate run of husbands could easily be due to widowhood and legal remarriage to successive brothers-in-law (parallel to the seven-time widow in Mark 12:18–23). Most importantly, Jesus makes no moral judgment about this woman, and neither should we.[6]

The point of the story is not her marital situation. Nor should the focus of the story be placed on any perceived wrongdoing on her part. Rather, Jesus shows himself as the Messiah. Jesus was an outsider in a place where Jews were clearly not welcome. Yet it was Jesus' desire to free the Samaritan people from their false idols and draw them into relationship with the larger community. He chose the woman at the well to collaborate in this important work. Jesus needs her to testify on his behalf!

Imagine what it was like for the Samaritan woman to hear Jesus tell her story. "[He] told me everything I have ever done!" (John 4:29). Everything. He told me everything. He told me the good, the bad, the confusing, the embarrassing, the profound and the joyful moments. He told me how all the pieces of my life fit together. He told me who I am, and what my life is all about. "He cannot be the Messiah, can he?" (John 4:29).

She has this encounter with Jesus, and she finds her voice! Jesus travels through Samaria, engages in conversation with this woman, and she becomes an unlikely messenger in an unexpected place. It is a story of transformation—a woman who was liberated and transformed by an encounter with Jesus. She is both worthy of the encounter with Jesus and open to the call to be one of his followers. Perhaps Jesus is calling women today to be leaders and bearers of God's message in unlikely places. God knows our stories, our culture and our questions. Jesus needs us to testify on his behalf in places where the word of God is not always welcome—courtrooms and country clubs; boardrooms and locker rooms; restaurants and bars; domestic violence shelters and juvenile detention centers. We don't have to be perfect. All we need is faith and a willingness to be the presence of love, healing and forgiveness for others.

The story of the Samaritan woman gives us a voice. It is the story of a nation, a culture, an entire people who were liberated and transformed by this relationship with Jesus. She shows how Jesus came for all people—Jews and Samaritans. Likewise, Jesus comes for each of us—women of all types—old and young, rich and poor, city dwellers and rural inhabitants, spiritual seekers and lost souls. It gives me great hope that Jesus' liberating word will continue to work through unlikely people and in unexpected places—even today.

FOOD FOR THOUGHT

1. What do you find interesting, exciting, confusing or challenging about being a young adult today? How do you respond to living in a high-tech, fast-paced world? Do you find yourself "in between" and in a hurry to get through it?

2. How would you describe your attitude toward faith (spiritual, religious, devout, searching, questioning, absent)? What questions do you have about your religious tradition and practices?

3. What are the profound questions you are asking right now in your life? Write some of them down. Post them in a place where you can see them and reflect on them on a regular basis.

4. Patience is a virtue in our fast-paced world. Practice creative loitering or lingering as a way of slowing down. Art galleries, coffee shops, parks, beaches, churches, forest preserves are all places made for lingering. Spend an hour or an afternoon with no agenda, other than to be present and pay attention.

CHAPTER TWO

• CAN YOU HEAR ME NOW? FINDING YOUR VOICE IN PRAYER •

How Shall I Pray?

How shall I pray?
  Are tears prayers, Lord?
  Are screams prayers,
    or groans
      or sighs
        or curses?
Can trembling hands be lifted to you,
  or clenched fists
    or the cold sweat that trickles down my back
    or the cramps that knot my stomach?
Will you accept my prayers, Lord,
  my real prayers,
    rooted in the muck and mud and rock of my life,
and not just my pretty, cut-flower, gracefully arranged
  bouquet of words?
Will you accept me, Lord,
  as I really am,
    a messed up mixture of glory and grime?
Lord, help me!
Help me to trust that you do accept me as I am,
that I may be done with self-condemnation

and self-pity,
and accept myself.
Help me to accept you as you are, Lord:
mysterious,
hidden,
strange,
unknowable;
and yet to trust
that your madness is wiser
than my timid, self-seeking sanities,
and that nothing you've ever done
has really been possible,
so I may dare to be a little mad, too.

—Ted Loder, *Guerillas of Grace* [1]

While growing up, my sister and I shared a bedroom and we kept a little routine each night before bed. After Mom tucked us in and the lights were turned off, we would spend some time talking about our day. Before too long, one of us would hush the other and say, "Shhh… I'm saying my prayers." A few minutes later the other would whisper, "Are you done praying yet? I have something else to tell you."

I don't remember what we talked about, nor do I recall the content of those prayers. I imagine that my evening prayer was some combination of the prayers I knew by heart (the Our Father, Hail Mary and Glory Be) and a spontaneous list of bedtime blessings (God bless Mom, Dad, Grandma, Grandpa...).

Sometime around middle school, when sibling rivalry got the best of us, we convinced my mom to let us have separate rooms. Actually, I insisted that I was moving out, even if that meant sleeping in the hallway! Thus, our days of sharing a bed (and our nighttime prayer ritual) were essentially over.

Years later, just before my sister left for college, we sat in her room listening to the popular song "Friends are Friends Forever." We played that song until the cassette tape was nearly worn and our friendship securely renewed. Today, we live in separate cities, so Becky and I talk on the phone every week. We talk about her kids, my students and our family. We long to see each other on holidays and special occasions. The conversation always ends by saying "I love you" and "I miss you." We've come a long way.

Bishop Robert Morneau says that prayer is "that basic communication between God and God's creatures that sustains and deepens a loving relationship."[2] My prayer has taken on many shapes and forms over the years, in the same way that my sister and I progressed from childhood make-believe to teenage angst to the easy flow of adult conversation. I still find comfort in the rote prayers that I memorized as a child. There is something very soothing about the feel of rosary beads wrapped around my fingers and the gentle rhythm of the Hail Mary. It's easy to fall back on the Our Father in times of crisis or on those nights when I'm too tired to come up with words on my own.

While our Catholic tradition contains many beautifully crafted prayers, our conversation with God does not have to be tied to a prescribed text. It is possible to connect with God at any time of day, using the words that naturally come to mind. Pausing to say thanks in a moment of gratitude can be prayer. There are days when I am overcome with awe at the sight of the sun rising over Lake Michigan and I am reminded that taking delight in God's creation is prayer. Some people like to sing their prayers, from classic hymns to contemporary praise. Even sappy love songs have a way of naming our joy, sorrow and heartache, so much that singing along to the radio can be prayer. I sometime scribble random thoughts onto Post-it notes and stick them in my journal as inspiration for writing, another form of prayer. The time we spend caring for those in need or consoling a friend reminds us of God's concern for us and all people. Action—the work of hearts and hands that draws us close to God through service and love of neighbor—is prayer.

As with any relationship, the words and gestures we use to express ourselves to God change and develop over time. During the young adult years, we move away or perhaps move home again. Our horizons broaden as we experience new places and new people, and we have a different outlook on life. We wonder, "God, why am I here? And where is my life headed?" As we find our place in the world, our needs and concerns begin to shift. Our deepest desires become clearer; we stumble over our own fears and failings and the demands we place upon God begin to change. The things we'd like to say to God are charged with excitement, anger, disappointment, gratitude, happiness, confusion, contentment and pain. Sometimes we're just not able to say what we need to say using the prayers we memorized back in the fourth grade.

Just as the relationship with my sister did not happen overnight, a relationship with God is created over time. Becky and I certainly had our share of fits and fights, and the closeness we feel today was created from a lifetime of shared experiences. Likewise, a relationship with God requires dedicated time spent together, and it is not always easy. Some of you may ask, "What if it's been a long time since I last prayed?" "What if I've never prayed," or "I don't know how to pray?" "What if I only pray when I'm in trouble or in pain?" "What if I'm in a slump, I'm angry with God, or some event in my life has drawn me away from prayer?"

Prayer is a lifelong conversation with the one who created us and loves us. We come to God in prayer as we are right now, not as we would like to be when we have it all together. Perhaps you might begin by talking to God about how you're feeling today and what is going on in your life in the present moment. I sometimes think prayer is like writing a letter to a friend with whom I haven't talked in a while. Sometimes I want to say everything, but I don't know where to start. Other times there is so much to say that I know one letter cannot contain it all. Begin with what is most important today; knowing that the conversation doesn't end when the period of prayer is over. I can pray again tomorrow, talk about the same concerns or new insights and continue the conversation. It is never too soon or too late to pray, and there is not one "right" way to approach God in prayer. God takes us where we are and helps us to move to the next step.

Prayer is that constant conversation and awareness of God, yet there are many things that keep us from prayer. We fall into the trap of thinking that prayer is reserved for the sacred space of a church sanctuary. Perhaps we want to wait until the right time of day, those minutes before your head hits the pillow, the weekend reserved for retreat or a day of reflection at church. It could be that perfectionism keeps us from praying. Thinking that I am not perfect enough or holy enough, or I don't have time to recite the perfect prayer, so I don't pray. Many days I find that I am just too busy and can't find time!

Spiritual writer Henri Nouwen puts it this way, "To pray, I think, does not mean to think about God in contrast to thinking about other things, or to spend time with God instead of spending time with other people. Rather it means to think and live in the presence of God."[3] He goes on to explain that while it is important to set time apart for God, we remove God from our daily life when we separate our thoughts into thoughts about God and thoughts about the people and events that occupy our everyday life. Prayer only becomes "unceasing prayer" (1 Thessalonians 5:17) when all of our thoughts—the pretty, ugly, pious or shameful—can be thought in the presence of God.

Prayer is a dialogue, not a monologue. God and I are both active participants in the conversation. We speak and listen, just as God listens and responds. Prayer is that intimate exchange between lover and beloved, the one we talk with like a best friend. God is the one to whom we direct our hopes and dreams and concerns for the world. God knows every bit of anger, frustration and confusion that we experience in life. In exchange, prayer is the path through which God conveys God's mercy and love. Prayer is one avenue through which we experience God's care, and one way of knowing God's dream for our life. As we discover this voice of friendship with God through prayer, it is a conversation that requires us to wait patiently, listen carefully and to speak the truth with courage.

Can We Talk? Claiming the Voice of Honesty

In many of my closest friendships, there has been a distinct turning point in the relationship. This has typically involved a moment of honesty in which one of us revealed something personal, humorous, embarrassing or painful—unsure of how the other might respond. Yet by taking this risk, we've gained an even deeper appreciation for one another.

I think about the first time my friend Joe shared his story of his journey to sobriety after years of destructive drinking. I remember when Karen told me the story of her unexpected pregnancy during college. I have several gay, lesbian and transgender friends, and I am so grateful for their willingness to share that part of their lives with me. In some cases, that has also meant witnessing the heartbreaking story of friendships and families torn apart by that same news. Likewise, all of these friends have carefully listened to my stories of overcoming obstacles in my own life. I can truly say that I love these people more for their vulnerability, and I am better able to trust them with my own problems and imperfections. Through prayer God invites us to that same kind of transparency.

In Psalm 139, the psalmist pays tribute to God, who knows our inmost thoughts and every action. God knows our successes and failures, our brokenness and best intentions, and God proclaims us wonderful!

> I praise you, for I am fearfully and wonderfully made.
> Wonderful are your works;
> that I know very well.
> My frame was not hidden from you,

when I was being made in secret,
intricately woven in the depths of the earth.
Your eyes beheld my unformed substance.
In your book were written
all the days that were formed for me,
when none of them as yet existed. (Psalm 139:14–16)

When we take an honest approach to prayer, we realize that we cannot hide from God. There is nothing that we can hide or need to hide. God knows everything about us. I used to find this very intimidating, as if Big Brother was somehow watching over my shoulder, ready to pounce on my every mistake. The thought that God knew every move I made was enough to make me self-conscious, if not paranoid.

Perhaps there is another way to think about this. Nothing we have is hidden from God, and there is no reason to try hiding things God. God is like the girlfriend who stops by unexpectedly when my apartment is a mess. Whether I am ready for company or not, she really doesn't mind. She already knows that I am far from perfect and insists on coming inside anyway. God is the one who comes over and sits on the bed, while I rush around picking up the clothes off the floor. She is more concerned about the conversation at hand than the dirty dishes in the sink. While she notices the dust on the shelves, she doesn't say anything about it, or she waits until just the right moment to gently say something.

It is comforting to know that I can be my true self in front of God, and that nothing I say or do will ever come as a surprise. God made us and knows us inside and out, with all our gifts and limitations, strengths and struggles. Approaching prayer in a spirit of honesty and truth is sometimes hard, because it requires that we be completely honest with ourselves. Prayer invites us to say out loud those things which God already knows to be true. It means that we must come to accept ourselves and acknowledge that God loves us just as we are. God loves all of the wonderful parts about us, and God continues to love us despite our weakness and shortcomings. As we grow in honesty, we see that God wants to be with us—always. It is in the mystery and messiness of life that we experience God's love and fidelity. God rejoices with us when there is cause for celebration, and God stands next to us when tragedy strikes.

As we allow ourselves to grow in honesty and transparency, we begin to see how God is constantly present and at work in our lives. An honest approach to prayer brings us back to the source of life and draws us to deeper dependence on God, knowing that our existence and purpose in life comes only with God's help. We begin to see God more clearly and understand who God is. As we become more open with God, we also open ourselves to God's response. We learn to trust God as a faithful friend and constant companion. As we reflect on life's joys and trials, we grow in understanding of God's deep regard for us. Our expressions of gratitude and forgiveness are a reflection of God's mercy. In prayer we place all our desires before God. We trust God with the people we love, with the sometimes inexplicable events of our lives and with all our plans for the future. As we allow ourselves to be known by God, our hearts are opened to all the possibilities that God has in store for us. Even our anger, anxiety and disappointment draw God into conversation and call God to accountability in the relationship. Together with God, we work to sustain and renew that relationship each day. Prayer strengthens us and prepares us to hear God's response.

I Can't Hear You! The Challenge of Listening
For some of us, there are days when prayer just feels right. Words of gratitude and praise flow easily, and conversation with God is comfortable and natural. If we are lucky, there are moments when we are overwhelmed with the feeling of God's presence, and we feel especially close to God in prayer. Occasionally, there are even times when deep insights rise up within us with great clarity.

One particular moment of clarity stays fresh in my mind. The summer after graduate school, life as I knew it quickly began to fade away. I sorely missed the daily interactions with classmates and professors.

Three of my long-time friends moved away, each to different areas of the country. My boss, who had been a valuable mentor, was unexpectedly transferred, and I began battling a knee injury from running. It seemed that every important relationship was dissolving, and even my primary outlet for recreation was being taken away. I went to Mass one Sunday and heard the familiar story of the multiplication of the loaves and fish (Matthew 14:13–21). As I reflected on Jesus feeding the crowd of five thousand people with only five loaves and two small fish, words welled up within me that said: "There will be enough." It suddenly put my entire situation into perspective. Just as there was more than enough food to feed a hungry crowd, I was assured that there would be enough sustenance in my own life. In this moment of prayer, I knew that there would be more friendships, other mentors and new opportunities. While it didn't change my situation or take away the pain, there was great comfort in knowing that God feeds all of our hungers—including my need for companionship, career advice and improved health. There would be enough.

Moments of intense prayer are a gift. They sustain us through extended stretches of mundane, ordinary, everyday life. The experience of knowing "there will be enough" kept me going through many months of job transition, physical therapy and personal growth. I am so grateful for this heightened awareness of God's presence. But having acute experiences is not always commonplace. Periods of darkness or confusion in prayer are not uncommon. They can be long, lonely and burdensome. Even the most fervent prayers experience moments of doubt and times of uncertainty. Haven't we all wished for God's response to be spelled out in words among the clouds and answers to come like flashes of lightening in the sky? Sometimes the hardest part of prayer is listening.

We live in a very noisy world. Our eyes and ears are filled with so many things. Music streams endlessly from our iPods, colorful billboards line the streets and hundreds of channels are just a click away on cable TV. How many times have I gone online to simply check *one* e-mail or look at tomorrow's weather forecast, and my attention is quickly drawn away by something else. It's a task that should take only a few minutes, and before I know it, I've spent a half hour surfing the Web. Surrounded by constant chatter, there is barely room to be still and it is nearly impossible to find silence.

I am fortunate to spend a week away on retreat every summer. I have been blessed to know the voice of God that wells up in prayer after several days of sitting in silence. Most people can't imagine an entire day of silence and resist the thought of going a week without e-mail or cell phones. I will admit extended periods of silence are not for the faint of heart! But the blessings that come from such time with God can be abundant and profound. Even five or ten minutes of silence each day are enough to center ourselves on God. Becoming more attentive to God in the silence is good practice for recognizing God in the busyness of our lives. In doing this, it is possible to train our hearts and ears to hear in new ways.

God is everywhere, and God is with us during every moment of every day. Sometimes we get so caught up in our own thoughts and our personal agendas that we don't even notice God is all around us. Making room for silence is a good way to take notice of God's presence. Try this simple exercise. Take five minutes at the end of the day to be by yourself. It might be late in the day, perhaps in the evening before going to bed. Find a quiet place to relax and just sit. Remember that God is present there with you. Think back on the events of the day. What sticks out for you? Was there anything important, significant, or noteworthy? It might be a conversation with a friend, a smile from someone at work, the laughter of a child or a favorite meal. Spend some time giving thanks to God for the special moments of your day. Talk with God about your feelings, actions and attitudes during the day. Where did you sense that God was moving, speaking and relating to you? Is there anything you need from God? As the day comes to a close, perhaps you might ask God for direction in life, strength during a particular hardship, clarity to make a decision, or the courage to seek forgiveness. You might like to finish this quiet time with the Our Father or praying aloud (or silently) in your own words.

This simple exercise of looking back on the day and acknowledging God's presence helps to strengthen our awareness of God's constant companionship. As you are able to name the ways in which God was present at the end of the day, you slowly begin to recognize God more regularly in the midst of the day. Listening for God while it is quiet becomes good practice for knowing God's presence in the hustle and bustle. Also, having a good guide (a spiritual director, favorite spiritual writer or interactive Web site) can make all the difference in the quality of your prayer. One Web site that many young adults have found particularly helpful is "Pray as You Go" (www.pray-as-you-go.org). It includes guided meditations, similar to the exercise described above, that you can download to your iPod or MP3 player.

One of the other challenges of listening is knowing when the "voice" we hear belongs to God. Even in the stillness, we replay conversations from our day. How do I distinguish God's voice from the never-ending committee meeting that rattles in my mind? How do I know it is God, and not my own personality pushing ahead, or my ability to self-doubt that is holding me back? It takes practice and careful attention to notice the difference. God's voice might be something we hear with our ears. God speaks through other people, like the encouragement of a friend who has known us for a long time. God also speaks in the quiet. God's voice is the tiny whisper that echoes deep within us, and it speaks with great clarity. We know it is God's voice because it "wells up" in other places.

In the story of Elijah from the first book of Kings, Elijah hides in a cave and is told to be ready for the Lord who will be passing by. As Elijah waits, there comes a strong wind, a rumbling earthquake and a blazing fire. But the Lord is not in any of these. After the fire there comes a tiny whispering sound. When he hears this, Elijah knows it is the voice of God. He hides his face in his cloak and goes to greet God at the entrance of the cave (1 Kings 19:9–15).

I often wonder what that tiny whispering sound was like. Was it a noise? Did it speak in words, and if so, what did it say? How did Elijah know it was God? Sometimes we expect to hear God speak with a big booming voice, but I think more often God speaks in the ordinary, simple moments when we least expect it.

My sister has many stories about the tiny whispering sound that comes from the mouth of her animated and energetic preschool-aged son. William is six, and he is always saying something outrageous or inspiring. One night William declared, "Moms and dads are the best thing in the whole world, except when they yell." Finding herself in a teachable moment, Becky explained to William that sometimes it is appropriate to raise our voices, like when you're trying to stop your little brother from running into a busy street. But sometimes we yell when we're upset, and we really need to talk things out instead. They came to the conclusion that families aren't perfect, and William seemed to understand. He looked at Becky and said, "Mom, you don't have to be perfect to be the perfect mom for me."

God often uses the people and experiences that are right in front of us to get our attention or to showcase God's affection and love. As Becky shared this story with me, she reflected on how hard it is to listen for the voice of God with three rambunctious kids running through the house. Moments like this remind her that God is present, even on those days when she is not at her best. Our awareness of God can be mediated by the concrete stuff available to us in the world, whether that is advice we receive from a friend, the beauty we see in nature, or something we hear on the evening news. It takes practice to hear God speaking to us. It requires us to pay attention to the world in which we live and creatively imagine the hand of the creator at work in all things. What if God is waiting to speak to us through music and movies? Imagine God using our conversation with family and friends to affirm our gifts and gently nudge us in new directions. Perhaps God works through our outrage with unjust systems to inspire us toward change. Could God be speaking to us in the voice of a stranger as we walk down the street? While it is sometimes easier to be attentive to God in the quiet, God also speaks to us in the busy moments of everyday life. If we pay attention, we quickly find that God is speaking all around us.

How Does God Answer Prayer? Waiting for God to Return Our Call

Last week I was on my way out to dinner with a friend, when I stopped at the ATM. I needed some money, and I was in a hurry. I inserted my card into the little slot, and without even thinking, I hit the "fast cash" option. No questions asked, just give me the money! The ATM gave me all these easy options: $20, $40, $60, $100, $200. After a few clicks, I was off to dinner. All of this without even talking to a real person! While I've grown accustomed to doing my banking electronically, when it comes to prayer, we cannot do it all on our own. Prayer is *not* like stopping at the ATM for fast cash. As much as I would like it, God does not spit back answers like a stream of twenty-dollar bills.

The greatest challenge of prayer is waiting for God's response. Can we dare to ask for what we need and what we believe is best, and yet remain open to God's wisdom? Are we able to surrender ourselves to God's timing? Do we give God the opportunity to reveal God's desire for us before acting on our own judgment? Sometimes life demands an immediate response. How do we make decisions, when there is no time to wait for clarity?

We are so steeped in a culture of immediacy. Like fast cash from the ATM, we want things *now*. We expect to see a response to a text message within minutes. Web page response times are measured in split seconds. It is easy to grow impatient. A friend of mine once suggested that if you want to learn patience, go to the grocery store to buy a single pack of gum, then stand in the longest checkout line.

Prayer often requires that we sit in the awkwardness and uncertainty of not knowing. It may take a long time. My idea of prayer and God's idea of a response may be completely different. We don't always get what we want or what we expect from prayer. Sometimes the answer is "no" and sometimes the answer is "not yet."

God answers prayer on God's own time and in ways we do not easily see. Prayer is as much about seeking as it is about finding. It is about paying attention and living in God's presence. Prayer is an invitation to openness, and it requires a healthy sense of detachment from the outcome. Having too many expectations puts limits on God and distracts us from what God needs us to hear. Yet not having any expectations doubts God's ability to move mountains and shower us with blessings. Prayer requires that we surrender ourselves to God's will and allow ourselves to be surprised by God's goodness.

Trust is essential to prayer, yet to live in trust is a huge challenge. God knows what God is doing, and God has our best interests in mind even if we cannot see it. We may not comprehend why God allows painful situations or why God does not grant us the things we legitimately desire. Real trust requires that we surrender our need for control, and it involves putting our confidence, our safety and our future in someone else's hands. There will always be circumstances in life that are beyond our control. Surrendering to anyone or anything beyond ourselves is scary, because we risk getting hurt or being disappointed. It may seem like a paradox, but the more we surrender our lives to God, the more clearly we see the good things God has in store for our lives.

My friend Ali is a great example of someone who, by listening and waiting, has learned to trust in God's goodness. Like many single people, Ali spent a long time searching for a soul mate. Her constant prayer was that God would bring her the perfect boyfriend and partner for life. About a year ago, finding herself on the single scene once again, Ali shared with me that her prayer had changed. Instead of praying for a relationship, she started praying for love. She prayed that God would channel her desire for a loving relationship to the place where God's love was needed most in the world. Much to her surprise, Ali has fallen in love with a wonderful organization that builds schools for children in India. It is the perfect match for her zeal for adventure travel, the peace she finds in Eastern meditation, and her adept skills in organizational development. Ali has visited their schools in India, and she has been instrumental in advancing their fundraising efforts in the United States. I have never seen her more happy or more free.

People often ask, "What do I do when I don't get what I prayed for?" I suppose the easy answer is to keep praying! The harder answer, however, is that sometimes there is no answer. We don't always get what we ask for in prayer. I'm not sure that God always gets what God wants either. Is it really what God wants when a parent falls ill or when a young person dies? How does God feel when a significant other breaks off the relationship or when a trusted colleague leaves the firm? Does God desire a world that is wrought with violence, hunger and injustice? There is no explanation when natural disaster strikes. We hear stories every day about the wrongfully accused being put to death and those seeking work who cannot find a job. Does God really want these things? No.

God gives us what we *need*, which is not always the same as what we *want*. God is not out to get us, but stands with us through the trials of life. No matter how much we pray for an end to violence or a cure for cancer, praying harder does not guarantee a positive outcome. Often our first reaction when tragedy strikes is to ask, "Why did this happen?" The deeper and more challenging question is, "How am I called to respond? What do I need from God right now? And what does God need from me in light of this situation?" In all our prayer, we must seek God's will and not our own. Prayer brings all of our challenges and burdens to mind, and prayer gives us the strength and courage to take action where God is asking us to care for the world. When faced with the unexplainable, prayer allows us to surrender those things beyond our control back into the hands of our gentle and loving God.

Prayer is a gift, and one that I hope you receive with joy. The young adult years are an important time to listen closely for God and give voice to the deepest longings of our hearts. The decisions that we make today will shape how we spend our time and the people with whom we share our lives for many years to come. The practices of silence, honesty, listening and waiting help us develop a lifelong relationship with God. As we become more attentive to God in the present moment, we will come to recognize God more easily and trust in God more readily throughout the rest of our lives. Prayer draws us into constant conversation with God. It takes the shape of memorized words and spontaneous exhortations. Prayer comes in the form of poetry, action or songs of praise. Prayer brings us comfort, and is an outlet in times of exasperation or unbelief. May you open the gift of prayer and find God waiting there.

FOOD FOR THOUGHT

1. How did you first learn to pray? What prayer styles/forms work best for you? How has that changed over time?
2. Think about a time when you were keenly aware of God's presence. Where do you most often see God and experience God's presence? Do you hear God speaking through the ordinary events of everyday life?
3. When is prayer easy for you? When is it difficult? What do you find most challenging about prayer? How do you persevere during periods of darkness or dryness in prayer?
4. Turn off your iPod, cell phone and other electronic devices and go for a walk. Look at people and smile. If the spirit moves you, say hello. See what happens.

CHAPTER THREE

• VOCATION: DISCOVERING THE VOICE OF THE TRUE SELF •

I...beg you to lead a life worthy of the calling to which you have been called.

—Ephesians 4:1

My Lord God, I have no idea where I am going. I do not see the road ahead of me.

I cannot know for certain where it will end. Nor do I really know myself, and the fact that I think that I am following your will does not mean that I am actually doing so. But I believe that the desire to please you does in fact please you. And I hope I have that desire in all that I am doing.

I hope that I will never do anything apart from that desire. And I know that if I do this you will lead me by the right road though I may know nothing about it. Therefore will I trust you always though I may be lost and in the shadow of death. I will not fear, for you are ever with me, and you will never leave me to face my perils alone.

—Thomas Merton, *Thoughts in Solitude*[1]

Birthdays are a wonderful time to take stock and give thanks for all that we are and all that we have accomplished in life. I distinctly remember the year my friends and I turned thirty. It seemed that our twenties were fraught with career changes, falling in and out of love and efforts to pay off college loans without falling deeper into debt. In typical young adult fashion, the twenty-something years were characterized by searching, seeking and self-discovery. For many of us, turning thirty was a chance to express our true selves, and we used this milestone birthday to proclaim our newfound identity.

Bridget, a freelance writer, hosted a party and invited her friends to bring their favorite piece of poetry or prose. Many of Wendy's friends are active in community theater, and they serenaded her guests with their favorite show tunes. An avid runner, Jenny celebrated her thirtieth birthday with a trip to Ireland, her family's country of origin, where she participated in the Dublin marathon.

The summer I turned thirty marked my first mission trip to Nicaragua. It was a celebration of my lifelong commitment to volunteer service and love for adventure travel. It was also the same year I left my career in corporate consulting to pursue a graduate degree in ministry. At the time, my heart and energy were divided between my consulting job and my volunteer pursuits. I felt like I was trying to be different things to different people. I found myself telling a friend, "I don't know who I am anymore. I just want to be *me*." Sensing my discontent she said, "You're looking for more than a new career, you're looking for a *vocation!*"

When we hear the word *vocation*, most people immediately think of marriage, priesthood and vowed religious life. But a vocation is more than one's marital status. It is an accumulation of skills, experiences and relationships which incline us toward a particular path in life. Our vocation is both a gift and a response to a call from God. It includes how we choose to spend our time, the people we enjoy and our response to the experiences and opportunities God places in our path. All that we have and all that we are is a gift from God. Just as God gives abundantly out of love, our vocation is a free response to God in love. God gives us the freedom to choose how we will spend our lives. We discover our true vocation to the extent that we discern wisely, exercise our freedom responsibly and choose what honestly seems to be the best course of action. Our vocation unfolds, and sometimes it finds us, as we continually respond to God's love through the choices we make.

I sometimes wonder about Jesus' life as a young adult. What kind of work did he do? Who did he meet, and how did they shape his life? What was his life like during those years? Sacred Scripture does not provide many details about his young adult years. The Bible summarizes Jesus' entire life, from the finding in the temple (traditionally age twelve) to his baptism at the Jordan River (around the age of thirty), with a single verse: "And Jesus increased in wisdom and in years, and in divine and human favor" (Luke 2:52).

Jesus' baptism at age thirty marks a turning point. It is from that point forward we begin to learn more about his life, ministry, work, teaching, healing, discipleship, encounters with authority and, eventually, his crucifixion and death. It is the moment of his baptism when Jesus comes into himself and realizes the fullness of who he is. "You are my Son, the Beloved, with you I am well pleased" (Luke 3:22). Jesus recognizes his call, the abundance of God's favor and the gift of God's love. This significant event does not make him into something he is not. Jesus has always been the beloved Son of God. Rather, this moment draws that truth into his consciousness. He understands more completely his vocation as a preacher, teacher, healer and one who is called to share God's divine love with the world.

Looking back on your life, was there a particular moment that confirmed that you were on the right path? It could be a promotion, a profound moment of prayer, an engagement or an affirmation from a complete stranger. Like Jesus, our young adult years are time to grow in wisdom and age, to increase in awareness of who God has called us to be, and understand more completely what it means to become ourselves. Whether you find yourself at age twenty, thirty or forty—the young adult years are the perfect time for exploration, self-discovery and a growing sense of confidence in the call.

Discovering your vocation is more than deciding what to do for a living. It is a way of being in the world. Every decision is an opportunity to say a deeper "yes" to God's invitation. Finding your vocation in life answers the questions: Who am I? Where am I going? Who is going with me? And how will I make a difference in the world?

Who Am I?

Who are you, really? There are so many ways to answer this question. We identify ourselves by our relationship to others. I am a sister, a daughter, a mother, a friend. We might respond with a job description, title or career field. I am a designer, an accountant, a teacher, a doctor. We identify ourselves by the organizations to which we belong or the pastimes we enjoy. The most extensive description might include personality traits, physical characteristics, marital status, nationality or religious affiliation. How would you answer the question, "Who are you?"

It takes a lot of confidence to be yourself in a world which tries to make us like everybody else. I received a lot of advice going into my first big job interview. Most people said, "Just be yourself." I imagine many of us have heard similar messages from parents, friends or trusted advisors. It is advice that is sometimes easier given than received. We all have a desire to belong, and there is a subtle temptation to conform to other people's expectations in order to be accepted. To land that first job, I spent hours polishing my résumé and formulating questions to show I had done my research. When it came to the interview, I was tempted to give answers that I suspected my new boss wanted to hear. I wanted them to see the real "me," but I also wanted to be accepted as one of "them."

It's not always easy to be yourself. We live in a competitive culture where marketing experts have convinced us that bigger is better and advertising sets the standard for success. It can be a real struggle to be true to yourself in a world where an ambiguous "they" define what is beautiful, successful and acceptable from what you wear to where you live and who you date.

Knowing ourselves, our identity and purpose in life, is the first step toward discovering our true vocation. God created each one of us different and distinct from all others, and each of us for a different purpose. As we begin to think about discovering God's dream for us, perhaps our first inclination is to quickly jump into questions about the ideal career or the person with whom to spend our lives. Vocation is not so much about "doing" as it is about being and becoming. It is about belonging to God.

The answer to "who are you?" rests partly in our response to the question, "whose are you?" First and foremost, we belong to God. The prophet Isaiah tells us that God has called us each by name, "you are mine" (Isaiah 43:1). Isaiah goes on to speak of God's constant care and protection. "When you pass through the waters, I will be with you; / and through the rivers, they shall not overwhelm you; / when you walk through fire you shall not be burned, / and the flame shall not consume you.... / Because you are precious in my sight /...and I love you" (Isaiah 43:2,4).

Our society is so caught up in doing and earning and succeeding. We sometimes forget that God loves us just as we are. It is OK to be "me." We forget that God's love is freely given and does not need to be earned. We don't have to buy it, and there is no need to conform to other people's expectations in order to receive it. Our vocation is shaped by our ability to receive life in gratitude and make a return to God with our lives. Our identity is God's gift to us, and what we become is our gift to God.

We are called to be holy. Holiness doesn't come from what we do; it isn't something we can earn. Holy is who we are (1 Corinthians 3:16–17). Holiness is something we already have. What makes us holy is our identity in Christ and knowing that we are God's beloved daughters and sons. Each of us is made in God's image and in God's likeness (Genesis 1:26). As we come into our own and become our true selves, we become a fuller image of God.

By becoming more of who we already are, we discover the unique person God created within us. We become humble. We don't always think of humility as a positive characteristic. Humility does not mean being passive, lowly, submissive or small. Humility is the ability to be who you claim to be. The opposite of humility is arrogance, boastful pride or to think of oneself as superior or inferior to others. The origin of the word *humble* (from the Latin *humus*) means to be close to the ground or of the earth. To be humble is to be grounded and rooted in our identity. Humility frees a person to be who they are, and in turn allows us to accept other people for who they are. To become humble is to know who I am and who I am not.

The humble woman lets her light shine! She will look at the opportunity for a promotion and say, "I've been the top sales representative for over a year. I know our clientele inside and out, and I think others can learn a lot from my experience. I'm committed to providing great customer service, and perhaps the best way to utilize my skills is by managing newer members of the sales team." Likewise she can also say, "I'm a good piano player, but I'm not meant to be a concert pianist. There is something very freeing about acknowledging that. It takes off the pressure to spend hours in rehearsal, and music becomes a joy when I'm asked to play for friends."

There is no right or wrong way to go about discovering who we are. We discover who we are by trying new things, paying attention to what feels right, naming things that we're good at, and listening for what other people affirm in us. It happens through prayer, reflection and by listening for the call from within. Finding our true self certainly does not happen without daring to dream and taking some risks. We are free to choose our own career, our friends, our interests. God leaves us free to be whatever we like. By becoming who we are in our fullness, we give glory to God.

This is not something that happens overnight. Becoming the person God wants you to be is something that unfolds over a lifetime. There is not one magic age where we wake up and discover that we have arrived at wholeness. Finding your vocation involves a lifetime of developing skills, acquiring experiences and engaging in relationships that form us and shape us. Becoming who God wants us to be is something that God is always doing, always creating and ever unfolding.

Where Am I Going?

My first grade teacher, Sister Floriberta, once said that the greatest sin (mistake) in life is to deny your vocation. I was convinced that Sister Floriberta was on a mission to make every girl a nun, and at age six, I wasn't sure yet what I wanted to be when I grew up. Nearly thirty years later, I'm still not sure what I want to be when I grow up. But having acquired an adult appreciation of vocation, I'd like to suggest a corollary to Sister Floriberta's statement. If the greatest mistake is to deny your vocation, then the greatest joy in life is to embrace your vocation. Knowing and following your true vocation in life is the path to ultimate happiness.

God wants us to be happy; God does not intend for us to be miserable. Likewise, God does not call us to things for which we are unfit or that are incompatible with whom we are. This does not mean that our work won't be physically draining or emotionally exhausting at times. It doesn't exempt us from the learning curve or from having a bad day. Ultimately, when our work is grounded in a sense of vocation, it leaves us feeling more alive, it brings more life to others and it draws us closer to God.

For many young adults, a great deal of time and energy is spent getting a career off the ground. We want our work to make an important contribution to society, but ideally we would also like it to be meaningful and purpose-filled. Our vocation in life rests at the intersection of our deepest desire and the world's greatest needs. Frederick Buechner puts it this way, "The place God calls you to is the place where your deep gladness and the world's deep hunger meet."[2] To the extent that you find this combination, it will give you energy and bring life to the world.

Discovering that place where deep joy meets deep hunger is not always easy and it is not a one-time decision. The Christian principle of discernment—intentional and prayerful decision making—acknowledges the presence and participation of something much bigger than us. Good discernment leaves the outcome open and in God's hands. Discernment is steeped in prayer, yet it needs a thorough knowledge of all the options available to us. Like a good decision-making process, we might weigh the pros and cons of a given situation. Discernment also implies that we take God's will for us into account, rather than simply our own needs and desires.

Discernment is the ability to respond freely to God's deep love for us. The world needs people who operate out of love. When we respond in love, it prevents us from making decisions primarily out of obligation or as a favor to someone else. As we listen to those who love us and know us well, they can help us name our gifts, passions and natural abilities. At the same time, it is essential that each of us follow the deepest desire and calling of our own heart. Someone who makes a decision out of guilt, fear, or need for approval may become resentful if things don't work out as planned. Worse yet, they may eventually find themselves waking up in someone else's dream. In good discernment, God's dream for our happiness becomes a dream that we share. You have to make this dream your own. The stories of two amazing women come to mind.

I recently met Janelle, a nineteen-year-old cancer survivor and college student, who has a real passion for science and research. She tells me that she never thought about going into medicine, but she is convinced that her journey through cancer treatment was not an accident. She says, "I know what a diagnosis of cancer does to an individual. And I wonder if God is inviting me to give something back to the cancer community." Grateful for her new lease on life, she is inviting input from others, reflecting on her experience and pursuing her academic interests. She has entered into the question about a career in medicine without forcing a decision or feeling obliged to go this route.

I also think about my friend Cathy whose parents encouraged her to get a four-year college degree. Unlike most of her classmates, she went off to college, and she was miserable! Within the first semester, she was physically sick from the pressures of college. While she feared that she would never live up to her parents' expectations, she finally admitted that the traditional college experience wasn't for her. She took a semester off, then enrolled in a local academy for hair design, and she eventually took some accounting classes at the local community college. She now has a steady client base and is getting ready to open her own salon. It is a profession in which she is truly happy and she finds great joy in her work.

As we consider God's will for our lives, it is not unusual to wonder if God has one particular plan in mind. Perhaps there is some mysterious treasure map hidden somewhere? And if I could just find this treasure map I would know which way to go. I would know the person I am supposed to marry, the job I am supposed to accept and the city in which I am destined to live. The will of God is not something that gets "beamed down" from heaven. We are not pawns waiting for God's almighty hand to move us around like pieces on a chessboard. God's plan for the world requires our active and conscious participation. We are participants in God's creative freedom. We have a choice in what we will become.

Some may ask: How important is the choice of what I do for a living? How much pressure should I put on myself to find the perfect job? What if my vocation (that which brings me joy and brings life to the world) is not the kind of career that puts money on the table? Or what if the job that I find myself doing in order to make a living is really not my true calling in life?

What we do for a living is important. We spend the majority of our waking hours working. Work assures our survival; it provides a source of income for food, shelter, clothing and leisure activities. Work also has the potential for providing great satisfaction and fulfillment in life through the relationships we build with colleagues or the service we provide to other people. However, no job is free from frustration, and there is a subtle temptation to define ourselves by our work. A person's job title or performance can become the measure of self-worth or value in life. When executives are focused solely on profit margins, it causes companies to lose sight of the dignity of their employees. The thought of going to work can be exhausting when we're met with increasing demands or the fear of losing our job.

Work is more than just making a living. Our work is a way of participating in God's creation. A stressful day can be tolerable when we truly believe in the mission of the organization. A special education teacher knows the nature of her job comes with some difficult moments, so she takes pride in the small successes of her students and keeps the wider vision of education in mind. Similarly, a strenuous job can be bearable when it is a means to a greater end. I once met a woman whose true passion in life is baking. Her dream is to open her own pastry shop, but due to financial constraints and family obligations, this likely will not happen any time soon. Meanwhile, she has an office job where she invests a lot of energy and does good work. But her career is not her life. Her real vocation comes at the end of the day—which includes loving her husband, raising a family, baking gourmet cupcakes for her son's birthday parties and preparing a Thanksgiving feast that rivals one from Martha Stewart.

Does God have a plan for my life? None of us can really know the answer to that question, but God promises not to abandon us in our pursuit. God is not going to leave us to our own defenses. God will put people and situations and opportunities in our path. God gives us everything we need to choose what is good. Discovering God's dream for our life can be scary. There is undue pressure to find the one right thing, but any decision we make is never the last decision. It is just the next decision. I don't have to worry about forever, if I am able to concentrate on doing the next right thing. Perhaps finding our vocation means making the best decision given everything I know up to this point.

I don't have to know everything the future holds, but fidelity requires that we remain in the conversation. Finding our calling requires risk. Our calling might look different than what we first expected. Discernment entails gathering information, using our imagination and sense of humor, engaging in conversation and asking a lot of questions. It takes patience and prayer, and perhaps a good mentor or spiritual guide. We need to be open, willing and able to move in whatever direction the Spirit calls us. Give yourself permission to be a beginner and be willing to make mistakes. At some point, finding our vocation requires that we take a leap of faith, trusting that God meets us even when we step into the unknown.

Who Is Going With Me?

God invites us to be with many different people over the course of a lifetime. Some are called to marriage or to the religious life, but others are called to be single.

While attending Catholic school, I heard a lot about vocations, but I have to admit the vocation to the single life was never given much credence. The idea that someone would intentionally choose to commit oneself to the single life was usually presented as a last resort when the other options didn't materialize. Yet for some people being single feels right in the same way that meeting the man of your dreams makes marriage the perfect path for others or still others feel most at home in religious life.

There are those who find themselves single while on their way to marriage, and others are single due to separation, divorce or the death of a spouse. There are also those who are single by choice—women and men who, with a sense of purpose and commitment, respond to God's loving invitation to remain open and unattached. Whether by choice or by circumstance, single people find themselves freed up for something else. This freedom may be directed toward friendship, to service, to hospitality or to other pursuits. In my own journey as a single person, I discovered that life was fuller and more complete once I made a conscious decision to stop dating. I was able to give myself whole-heartedly to my friendships and volunteer activities, and I was free from the anxiety heaped upon me by the expectation that I should be married.

For those who truly desire to be married, the single years can be a lonely and frustrating time. We all experience loneliness. Loneliness exists within a marriage, and the structure of community life can cause isolation for vowed religious. Single people too have their own kind of loneliness. There is a subtle temptation to quickly fill that space with work, entertainment or other excesses. Finding creative ways to channel loneliness can be a real gift when we use that space for personal growth or by creating a safe place for others to enter into our lives.

In her wonderful article "Singleness and Spirituality," Francine Cardman notes,

> Where singleness is acknowledged and respected, however, it can be a sign and a service to the whole community. It is a sign of hope and hospitality, of friendship and of waiting on God. In its essential openness, the single life is a reminder of the pilgrimage that we are all on as the people of God.[3]

Whether we find ourselves temporarily single, single again after death or divorce, or single for a lifetime—it is enough to be single and to be open to whatever opportunities present themselves. Holiness, happiness and fulfillment are available regardless of our vocation.

All people are called to be in relationship with one other. We are not meant to be alone; our lives are inherently relational. We are surrounded by a community which includes our family, friends, neighbors, clients, classmates and work colleagues. These people are instrumental in helping us develop as persons, and they help answer the vocation question. Part of discovering your vocation means exploring two key questions: Who do I want to be with? And how do I want to be with them?

We can think about these questions in the context of our career and our personal life. Someone entering a health care profession might consider, "Do I want to be with people who are sick or injured, and can I be with them in such a way that leads to their physical healing?" Someone called to teaching might ask, "Can I give myself to people in such a way that leads to their greater understanding of a particular subject area, and do I feel called to share my knowledge with children, adolescents, adults?" Someone who is discerning marriage might want to consider, "What expectations do I have of this other person, and what qualities do I bring to the relationship? Do I desire to have children? How much time to be alone do I need?"

The vocations of marriage, religious life and single life invite us to make a commitment to be with another person or group of people. Commitment requires tremendous courage and willingness to give oneself completely to others, whether that commitment is to a family, a faith community or single persons who give themselves fully to friendship, family, work and other communities. In all cases, genuine commitment leads to greater freedom and wholeness.

On the surface, commitment and freedom seem like contradictory values. Freedom implies keeping all of our options open, and commitment involves closing off options in order to make one clear choice. In this way, commitment is often seen as restricting our freedom. But consider freedom in another way. The freedom to vote is meaningless, unless we commit to a particular candidate. In the same way, the freedom of speech does nothing if we remain silent or abuse it. But it becomes a powerful tool when we take a stand on an issue. Freedom and commitment are complementary, not contradictory.

In the context of vocations, a commitment of any kind—to being single, married or religious—opens up a deep freedom. Freedom is the abiding sense that we are loved and accepted, which allows us to make choices consistent with God's call. Given this freedom, commitment is an expression of surrender and trust. Any commitment made in love draws us into deeper trust, relieves us from fear and leads to freedom.

A vocational commitment makes a person free to live as God intends. By doing so, we become more fully ourselves; we become whole.

Many young adults see their single years as a time of waiting to get married. Society views marriage as "normal" or "right," and tells us that if we are not married we have somehow failed. Relationships fulfill our desire for companionship and intimacy, but we can fall into the trap of believing that another person will complete us. We put our lives on hold until we meet the person who will become our "other half." Wholeness is not something we get from someone else. Single people often find fulfillment through their friendships, careers or volunteer commitments. Even in marriage, one person cannot respond to all of our needs. For these reasons, we relish the presence of extended family, colleagues and friends.

Wholeness comes from God and from our relationship in Christ. A complete life is one in which all of our decisions and relationships have the potential of calling us to a deeper relationship with God. As we contemplate our direction in life, another good question to ask is, "Will this person bring me closer to God? How will I help this person to become closer to God?"

Adhering closely to God is more than an invitation to regular prayer or church attendance. It is about the people who surround us in the ordinary circumstances of everyday life. Am I surrounded by loving people who point to God's presence? Do my friends encourage one another to live with integrity? Do they help me develop a deeper sense of virtue in my own life? I think about friends of mine who are married with young children. David takes prides in the way Nancy keeps him calm in situations when he would otherwise lose his patience. One of my colleagues has a wonderful sense of humor, and her joyful presence immediately puts people at ease. My friend Steve, a social worker, has many clients who suffer from mental illness. His strong example of compassion is one that I try to emulate in my own encounters with people who are struggling. Each of them, by their presence and example draw me closer to God.

Sometimes we choose the people who are going with us on the journey. Other times they find us and follow along the way. Friends may come and go, while siblings, a spouse or children are with us for a lifetime. Whether we choose to be married or remain single, we are surrounded by people. Some of them comfort and challenge us; others will anger and irritate us. Each one has the potential for calling forth a deeper relationship with God.

How Will I Make a Difference in the World?

God gives each of us unique set of skills, talents and abilities. Some talents reveal themselves naturally at a young age, as in the way some people are born with the ability to play a musical instrument. Other skills are developed with years of practice, like the incredible patience of my high school guidance counselor. God sometimes gives us gifts we think we don't need for reasons we don't completely understand. Part of discovering our vocation, our true selves, is growing to appreciate and understand the gifts we've been given.

Try this simple exercise: On a piece of paper write down six of your gifts that you value and consider important. Do not to limit yourself to occupational skills, but also include personality traits and other positive qualities. What do people affirm in you? What are you good at? What gives you joy and makes others happy?

God delights in having us use our gifts to become the person who God created us to be. Like presents beneath the Christmas tree, the gifts we receive from God are meant to be given away. God is always inviting us to share our gifts with those around us. By naming and accepting our gifts, we come to realize how each of us can use our gifts to make a difference in the world.

Several years ago, some members of our church were preparing for our annual service trip to Nicaragua. We knew that the schools we planned to visit were located in one of the poorest areas of Central America, so we developed a list of items to bring along including games, books and school supplies. Hoping that all of these items would be put to good use, we called the volunteer coordinator and asked what else we could bring. She said, "While all of the items on your list would be appreciated, I would really encourage your group to spend some time discerning your spiritual gifts."

We were all a little dumbfounded by that response. We were so excited about the material things that we missed thinking about what it would mean to use gifts such as compassion, encouragement, teaching, administration and leadership. During the few weeks remaining before our trip, we spent some time reflecting on Scripture and discerning the gifts of the Holy Spirit (Isaiah 11:1–3). It was an important lesson for all of us, because some of the most important gifts were the ones that took up no additional space in our luggage.

The kids were delighted with craft projects and new soccer balls, but the real success of the trip was measured by what we gave spiritually. Paula spent hours reading to the kids in Spanish. She made many new friends with her patience, time and attention. Holly has the gift of healing, always ready to share an encouraging word or her secret remedy for an upset stomach. And Ali has this incredible ability to keep people organized with her attention to detail and travel logistics. We literally would have been lost without her!

Our Catholic faith gives us many references to spiritual gifts. There are seven gifts of the Holy Spirit: wisdom, understanding, counsel, fortitude, knowledge, piety and fear of the Lord. In addition Scripture lists the gifts of faith, healing, mighty deeds, prophecy, discernment of spirits and varieties of tongues (1 Corinthians 12:4–11). There are those with gifts for teaching, generosity, leadership, mercy and hospitality (Romans 12:4–18). Ephesians goes on to list various roles in ministry such as apostles, prophets, evangelists, pastors and teachers (Ephesians 4:11–12).

Too often when we think about finding our vocation, we immediately jump to a job description or our state in life. Success by godly standards is also measured by how we use our gifts—whether we use them to pursue a career, leisure activities, artistic expression or volunteer endeavors. When we consider our spiritual gifts, we begin to see the fuller picture of our vocation. It is not only what I do for a living, but who I am at the core of my being. It is *all* of who God made me to be.

Our vocation is a lifelong journey of people, places, decisions and dreams. There will be times when everything seems to be going our way, and other times when it feels like we just can't get a break. At times we will find ourselves on the fast track, and then, to our chagrin, life takes us on one long detour. In a particular way as young adults, our lives are unfinished. We are always incomplete, yet every situation has the potential for calling forth goodness in us. Much of life still lies ahead of us. How will you know when you have arrived? What will it look like? How do you define success?

Success by worldly standards is easily measured by the amount of "stuff" we have acquired or the places and people with whom we spend our time. Our U.S. culture typically defines success in measurable quantities, where a higher number equals a larger rate of achievement including salary, stock shares, value of my 401(k) or the number of minutes available on my cell phone plan. Having money to pay the bills and saving for retirement are not bad things. For many people, success comes from knowing that I can pay for my kids' college education or spend time traveling during retirement. Success is also measured in the value of relationships, time spent with people we love, and the joy that comes from knowing I've made a difference for someone else. With all of life's twists and turns, success comes from finding contentment and peace, even in the face of fear or anxiety. It is about trusting that all will be well, even when things are not going well.

In the "Principle and Foundation" of the Ignatian *Exercises*, Saint Ignatius says,

> We should not fix our desires on health or sickness, wealth or poverty, success or failure, a long life or a short one. For everything has the potential of calling forth in us a more loving

response to our life forever with God.

Our only desire and our one choice should be this: I want and I choose what better leads to God's deepening life in me.[4]

You may want to pause here and read that paragraph again. This is a very hard saying. Ignatius firmly believed that God is involved in every detail of our lives. Our work, health, relationships, successes and failures are all gifts from God. All these things have the potential of directing our attention toward God's action in our life. Ignatius' statement is not meant to be a justification for poverty, sickness or hardship. It does not mean that we should not strive for a better life for ourselves and others. Indeed, we should work hard to enhance the life and dignity of all people and seek those things that lead to wellness and a long life. God wants to give us all good things. When Ignatius says that our only desire should be those things that draw us closer to the Lord, he suggests we maintain a "holy indifference" to health or sickness, wealth or poverty, death or life. Wherever we find ourselves, therein lays the potential for life with God.

I think about a couple who was confronted with unsettling news following a routine ultrasound. Despite what seemed like a normal pregnancy, their infant daughter was diagnosed with severe birth defects and underdeveloped organs. Her chances of survival were slim. They spent countless hours consulting with doctors and weighing all their options. Even with the best medical attention, they needed something short of a miracle in order for her to survive. When asked what they planned to do the couple responded, "She is ours, and we will love her as best we can for as long as she is here." When the due date finally arrived, they delivered a beautiful baby girl. She lived for fourteen minutes. The impact of that one life lasts forever.

This tiny and imperfect body was met with God's perfect grace. Her parents continue to count the blessings of this time. They experienced an outpouring of support from family, friends and doctors who held onto hope against all odds. They realized how much they care for one another and learned to comfort one another despite unspeakable grief and loss. They were strengthened in their desire to raise a family—fully knowing the joy, struggle and heartache that would accompany their dream to be parents. The gifts they received were beyond anything they had imagined.

Consider the circumstances of your own life. Where is God present? Are you grateful even when things aren't going as planned? How do you hold onto "holy indifference" in your career, relationships and personal life? Do you make decisions that lead you closer to God? Do you have desires that draw you away from God? Are there things in life you could live without? In the end, what do you think makes you successful?

For Christian believers every aspect of life can be related to God. All things come from God including our success, failure, sickness and health. God calls us to be faithful through it all. Hanging on to fidelity and trust in the midst of a busy life is a challenge, especially in a culture that puts a lot pressure on us to earn more and have more and do more. Where are you going? Who is going with you? How will you make a difference? We revisit those questions throughout our lives. Sometimes the answers are right in front of us. Other times they take years and years to unfold. Circumstances change and new opportunities will cross our path. Our vocation is not a one-time decision. It is a lifetime of saying "yes" to God.

FOOD FOR THOUGHT

1. Take some time to reflect on these four questions: Who am I? Where am I going? Who is going with me? How will I make a difference? Which question was the easiest to answer? The most difficult? Can you identify one thing you want to work on in the month ahead?

2. Take a piece of paper and write down all of the "roles" you play. Consider how each of them helps identify who you are and how you are to be in the world. Are there roles you don't like? Roles that you feel are forced on you?

3. Consider your spiritual gifts. Read 1 Corinthians 12:4–11 or Romans 12:4–18. Reflect upon the biblical spiritual gifts and also how you might share your gifts with others.

4. Reflect on the hidden young adult years of Jesus' life (Luke 2:52). Ask Jesus what his life was like during this time. Tell Jesus your story and how you arrived at the place you are today.

5. Make a list of 100 things you want to do before you die—from the serious to the silly, but all within reason (such as, "I want to get married." "I want to have children." "I want to fly in a helicopter." "I want to go deep sea fishing off the coast of New Zealand." "I want to learn another language.") Do you notice any trends? What do they tell you about your deep desires in life? Give yourself permission to do some of these things!

CHAPTER FOUR

• I'LL BE THERE FOR YOU: THE VOICE OF FRIENDSHIP •

Pleasant speech multiplies friends,
    and a gracious tongue multiplies courtesies.
Let those who are friendly with you be many,
    but let your advisers be one in a thousand.
Faithful friends are a sturdy shelter:
    whoever finds one has found a treasure.
Faithful friends are beyond price;
    no amount can balance their worth.
(Sirach 6:5–6, 14–15)

A regular group of us used to get together on Thursday night to watch the TV hit show *Friends.* In the ten-year stretch that *Friends* was on the air, viewers watched a cast of six friends support one another through life's tenuous moments as they crossed the threshold from their late-twenties into their mid-thirties. We witnessed the highs and lows of their budding careers, romantic relationships and interpersonal struggles. *Friends* made us laugh and cringe at the same time. It was like watching our lives unfold on television. We could all relate to being set up on a blind date, preparing our first Thanksgiving dinner, crying on a roommate's shoulder after a botched job interview or having a crush on the guy who lived in the apartment across the hall.

For a half hour each week, my friends and I imagined that our living room was the Central Perk coffee shop where the friends gathered, comedic drama unfolded and life happened in humorous sound bites. And of course, we all knew the words to the familiar theme song "I'll Be There for You" by the Rembrandts.

There is nothing like a good friend to brighten a rainy day. Friends are there for us when we've had a breakup, an injury, or a major disappointment. I can borrow her clothes and trust her advice on romantic relationships. A friend is someone with whom we can celebrate our accomplishments and grieve our losses. Friends give us space when we need to be alone, and they show up in the moments when we really need someone to be there. Friends make us laugh, help us cry and remind us that everything is going to be OK. Our friends are the ones who have seen us at our best and worst, and they like us anyway.

Friends know the most intimate details of our lives. There is a sense of completeness when someone knows us inside and out. Our friends remind us—with all our achievements, eccentricities and even the times we have fallen short—that we are cherished and appreciated by someone else. We all need someone who will affirm our ambitions, call out our bad habits, challenge our crazy ideas, acknowledge our deepest longings and understand our darkest hurts. It is a gift to have someone like this in our lives. We all have a desire to be known. It is a most basic human longing, this desire to be intimate with another, and to be known at the core of our being. This knowledge goes beyond the superficial facts of life and into the deep mysterious places of the heart.

Young women rely on their friends more than ever as they discover their own inner strength and learn to stand on their own. Friends are some of the most important people during these formative years. Friends walk side by side with us as we cross the threshold from living at home, to finding our way in the world and perhaps starting a family of our own. With young adults marrying later in life, friendships are essential to an active social life, an engaging work life and a devoted faith life. Over the last twenty years, the median age of marriage has risen for both men and women.[1] An extended circle of friends becomes like family during the young adult years. They are with us to celebrate birthdays, spend vacations together and relax over a holiday weekend. Their opinions influence our decisions and shape our values. Friendship provides safety in numbers, trusted advice for advancing careers and a creative outlet for recreation and fun. They care about us personally and professionally, and they promise to catch us if we fall. They remind us that we are loved no matter what happens and help us move forward with our lives.

Friendship in a Fast-Paced World

At a time when technology often takes the place of face-to-face communication, friendship has taken on an interesting new dynamic. The cell phone in my pocket vibrates, and I know immediately from the caller ID that it is my sister who lives 500 miles away. Without hesitating, I excuse myself from a table full of friends to spend a few minutes catching up with her. Although she frequently sends e-mail messages and pictures of her kids, it is a real treat to have a live conversation. No one at the table seems to mind, and as I return someone else appears to be checking their phone for sports scores, stock prices or text messages. It is not uncommon to have a conversation with the person sitting in front of us while simultaneously checking our electronic gadgets.

Technology, once considered the wave of the future, is here. Young adults in their late thirties welcomed the dawn of the computer era, while today's teens and twenty-somethings can hardly imagine a world without e-mail, cell phones, digital cameras and laptop computers. We live in a fast-paced world where people are constantly coming and going, and electronic tools allow us to stay in contact with more people across wider geographic distances. High-speed connections enable us to stay in contact with people who would have otherwise fallen off the map of our lives. High school classmates or college roommates can go separate directions but are only a click away. Technology is a great way to keep in touch with friends who live elsewhere or reconnect with people we haven't seen in a long time. Likewise, e-mail and online communities create a network of people with whom we can stay connected during life's transitions.

At the same time, I wonder about the quality of friendships that are developed and maintained through electronic means. There are endless opportunities for virtual friendships through social and professional networking Web sites and online dating services. In what sense can we also call these people our "friends"? Are online friendships different from friendships that were started and maintained face to face?

In many ways, building and maintaining a friendship is easier with the help of technology. Electronic forms of communication increase the speed and ease of staying in contact with others and minimize the distance felt by those who are far away. Some people prefer to gather their thoughts before putting them in writing, and find that they are able to express themselves more completely in a written format. Technology provides important assistance for those with physical impairments such as speech disorders or hearing deficits, helping to improve communication and reduce the level of disability that people with these conditions experience. Technology also provides a means for getting to know others (such as those seeking potential employment or romantic interests) before actually meeting them in person.

Virtual communication also presents its share of challenges. While not always ideal, some people use technology to avoid uncomfortable or awkward situations. Perhaps it is easier to leave a message rather than speak in person to a grieving friend. A significant other may choose to break up over e-mail rather than confront what went wrong in the relationship. On one hand, technology reduces some of the emotional barriers, but it also removes the personal element. Words can be misconstrued or taken out of context, while certain expressions (like humor and sarcasm) are often difficult to translate. Meanwhile, non-verbal cues such as tone of voice, facial expression, pace of words and body language are completely lost. There is an emotional bond created when you can read another person's body language, share silence face to face, or respond with a gentle touch or a simple smile. As one of my friends noted, after an unpleasant experience with online dating, technology makes it tempting for people to stretch the truth when describing their personality or physical attributes. We wonder if the "real" version will be the same as the person we perceive over the phone or online.

Will You Be My Friend? Qualities of a Good Friendship

Who are your friends? What qualities do you most appreciate about them? What makes one person a friend and another just an acquaintance? Some responses might include: "I've known this person a long time." Or, "This person knows me really well. We live in the same neighborhood and share a lot of things in common. We hang out together socially, or we go to the same church." Why do some friends stick together while other relationships fall apart? After spending so much time together, do you ever look back and ask, "How did we become friends in the first place?"

Friendship generally begins when two people share a similar experience. Perhaps you remained in contact with your best friend from kindergarten, the randomly assigned college roommate, or people you've met through travels or work. In his book *The Four Loves,* C.S. Lewis dedicates a chapter to "the happiest and most fully human of all loves"—friendship.[2] Lewis notes,

> Friendship arises out of mere companionship when two or more of the companions discover that they have in common some insight or interest or even taste which the others do not share and which, till that moment, each believed to be his own unique treasure (or burden). It is when two such persons discover one another …that friendship is born. And instantly they stand together in an immense solitude.[3]

While friendship begins when two people discover they share a common insight or interest, friendship grows beyond the initial contact to include other aspects of our lives, and the best friendships continue regardless of the event that first brought us together. True friends do more than just rehash old times, and it takes more to maintain a true friendship than occasionally "catching up" on our separate lives. Friendships deepen when you deliberately spend time together. Friends create shared memories together, and they choose to have new experiences for the sake of building and maintaining the friendship.

There is an unwritten rule in my family that says, "You can choose your friends, but family is forever." While it was always expected that I would have a close and loving relationship with my brothers and sisters, it is the *intentional* nature of friendship that solidifies that bond. Family and friend relationships are sometimes fraught with pain and conflict and irresolvable tensions. When we choose to be friends, we accept the joyful moments as well as the embarrassing episodes.

I remember the year I spent Thanksgiving with my best friend Bridget and her family. It was one of those less-than-perfect family gatherings where everyone seemed to get on each other's nerves, and we left shortly after dessert was served. As we started the drive home, Bridget began to cry. I was at a complete loss for words, so I slipped a CD into the car stereo and hit the repeat button on our favorite song. She cried while I drove, and neither of us said a word the entire ride home. As we turned toward her apartment, Bridget wiped away a few final tears. I apologized for not having the right words to say. She sighed and said, "It's OK. I just needed someone to be here, and you hold space really well."

A friend is one who knows the deepest truth of our life and loves us for who we are. Friends help us grow in authenticity. I find that I can genuinely be "me" when I am with my friends. There is no need to hide my flaws, fake how I'm feeling or try to impress my friends. Over the years, I have also found that friends complement each other well. There are parts of me that only some other friend can fully bring to light. I tend to be an introvert and a meticulous planner, so it's no surprise that most of my friends are great conversationalists and much more spontaneous. When we are together, we bring out the best in one another.

Ideally, friendship is also based in equality. We might have different interests, opinions, or approaches to life, but somehow we are able to keep the relationship on equal footing. We value one another to the same degree, and we carry a similar balance of emotional investment in the relationship. Just because one person has more money, talent or experience it does not get in the way of the friendship. For example, my friend Rebecca knows a lot of people! Yet I never feel out of place when I am with her, because she always makes a point to introduce me to other people and draws attention to the interests we have in common. My friend Abby speaks with great passion about her work as a speech-language pathologist (something I know nothing about!), and she graciously answers even the simplest questions. I have another friend who makes a significantly higher salary than I do. She will sometimes pick up the tab for dinner on special occasions, but if we're splitting the bill I trust that she's not going to invite me out to a restaurant that I cannot afford.

A sense of equality adds great value to friendship. Meanwhile, nothing is more awkward than lopsided friendships. There is the friend who demands a lot of my emotional energy without reciprocation, the friend who invokes feelings of guilt when I choose to spend time with other people, or the friend who relentlessly tries to trump my arguments when we talk about politics. Genuine friends don't keep score, but desire what is good for the other and for the relationship. There is a high degree of mutual respect and a fair amount of give and take. True friends want what is best for the other and take joy in another person's success. Each one seeks the good of the other, not out of self-interest, but for the greater fulfillment of the other. This is the difference between a friend and an acquaintance. Acquaintances may have shared interests, but there is no investment in the relationship simply for the sake of the friendship. Instead, the relationship is based on self-seeking interest or one shared activity.

In true friendship, I want that which is best for my friend, even if I get nothing in exchange. Friendship makes demands on us. There are times when we must give without counting the cost, knowing that there will be no benefit in exchange. The good of the other person is itself a reward. There are the demands of caring for a sick friend or individuals who pour out endless amounts of support for a friend with a sick child. I have a friend who endured a painful separation, and for many months I listened patiently even though the conversation always centered on her. We put our best foot forward for our friends, knowing that there are some cases in which we stand to gain nothing for ourselves. I think about the time I wrote a letter of recommendation for a friend, even though I knew she would move away if she was offered the job. Another friend cut off contact for nearly six months while she was seeking treatment for an addiction. When we get together now, I refrain from ordering a glass of wine with dinner. It is a small sacrifice to make, but it reminds me that I stand in solidarity with her desire to remain sober. When we want the best for our friends, it requires that we sometimes put our own needs and desires aside.

One of the greatest challenges of friendship is that friends are not always permanent like family, spouse or siblings. We do not take vows and there is no public commitment. Rather, friendship is based in mutual trust. The expectations about what one hopes for or needs from the relationship often go unspoken. Whether we tell this person our deepest secrets or ask them to take care of our cat while we're on vacation, friendship requires a certain level of trust and acceptance. Sooner or later friends may fail us, and we realize the other person has imperfections and limitations, just like we do. There are times when it may be best to break off a friendship, although we cannot give up on our friends without good reason. More often, we find that friendships simply wear out. The attraction that first brought us together has worn thin. One friend moves to a new city, we move on to new activities, or we no longer find substance beyond the initial contact.

In some ways our friends never leave us. They influence our attitudes and behaviors, and they shape our lives with the lessons they bring. I have a lot of friends who have come and gone in my life. I have friends from high school and college whom I rarely see, but we still exchange Christmas cards every year. There are other friendships that were intensely personal and meaningful for a year or two, but for a variety of reasons we've gone our separate ways. Each one made a huge difference during a particular time of my life. Friends leave an imprint on us. Even if a friendship ends, we can continue to glean wisdom from the people who move in and out of our lives.

Friendships don't have to end when someone moves, gets married, or when a significant life change occurs. Like any relationship, friendships change over time, just as we change with time. We develop new interests, our attitudes and opinions shift, and life circumstances may pull our time and attention away from the friendship for awhile. In order for the friendship to survive, it requires an acceptance of each other's situation, an openness to new adventures together and gratitude for what the other person brings to the relationship. Most importantly, it requires that we appreciate the other *person* as much as we enjoy the activities we share in common. In true friendship, if the factors that brought us together are taken away, we will still have a reason to be together and still enjoy one another's company. There is always room for growth in friendship, and the best friendships grow deeper and stronger with time. As long as we remain open, we never stop finding new friends.

Jesus as a Role Model for Friendship

At the end of Matthew's Gospel, Jesus promises, "And remember, I am with you always, to the end of the age" (Matthew 28:20). I find great comfort in this simple statement and knowing that Jesus is always with us. A friendship with Jesus is truly a friendship like no other. We sometimes don't think about Jesus in the same way that we think about our face-to-face friends. Is Jesus someone with whom you intentionally choose to spend time? Is this someone with whom I can talk about my day, share secrets, or ask advice on relationships? How is a friendship with Jesus similar to the friendships I have in person? How is it different? What expectations do we place on our relationship with him? What does a genuine friendship with Jesus require of us?

Perhaps we find it difficult to think about Jesus as a friend. He lived so long ago. How could he possibly understand what it is like to be a young adult today? Jesus was perfect, after all he is God! Why would he want to be friends with someone like me? Jesus, our mighty Savior, seems untouchable and far superior to anyone I would choose as a friend. Perhaps we keep a certain distance out of fear of what a friendship with Jesus might require of us in return.

A friendship with Jesus is indeed different than our face-to-face friends. The way we experience the presence of Jesus is not the same as the way we experience a friend sitting next to us on the sofa. Like a long-distance relationship, a friendship with Jesus transcends our ability to touch the other person and see them in real life. Like our face-to-face friendships, getting to know Jesus requires some shared experiences, some honesty, some trust, some vulnerability and some dedicated time spent with one another. We get to know Jesus through prayer, we learn about his life by reading Scripture, and we connect with him through the sacraments.

God became a human being in the Person of Jesus—fully divine and yet fully human. Like a friend who knows us inside and out, Jesus knows what it is like to be one of us. Jesus, because he was a human being, understands the human experience. It is a common bond that we both share. I think about the times I've sought advice from a close friend. I usually spend a lot of time explaining the situation, uncovering my motivations and rationalizing why I did or said certain things. When I bring these things into prayer, Jesus understands. He's been there. He gets it.

I think about the face-to-face friendships that have meant the most to me. I recall the easy flow of conversation, the intimacy of sharing secrets, a growing sense of trust in one another and bearing the gentle yoke of forgiveness. There are many Gospel stories where we find these same attributes in Jesus and his friends. One story in particular illustrates this point quite well.

In John's telling of the Last Supper, he includes an episode in which Jesus washes his disciples' feet (John 13:1–20). Washing feet was a grimy and dirty job. Feet clothed in sandals quickly gathered mud and filth after a day spent walking along the dusty roads. A host would typically offer a towel and water in order for weary travelers to wash their feet. It was such degrading work that slaves were not even required to perform such a service. And yet Jesus submits himself to this chore.

Imagine Jesus washing your feet. There is a reason we keep feet hidden beneath socks and protected with hard-soled shoes. Perhaps only someone who regularly gives or receives pedicure treatments can imagine what Jesus sees. One cannot wash another's feet without getting up close and personal. What Jesus uncovers can be dirty, smelly and gross. He discovers the parts of our life that are blistered and calloused, warped and wrinkled, swollen and bruised. By washing his followers' feet, Jesus is willing to look at the less-than-pretty side of life. I imagine the intimacy of touching, the sensitivity of someone who is ticklish, the exchange of words and the refreshing feeling of clean feet. In this gesture of friendship, Jesus distinguishes himself as someone who knows the deepest truth of our life and loves us anyway.

By washing his disciples' feet, Jesus expresses his desire to put their relationship on equal ground. Jesus becomes both servant and leader. He deliberately reverses his title of teacher and Lord and humbles himself to a subordinate role. "I do not call you servants any longer…I have called you friends" (John 15:15). He does not allow power, authority and social status to get in the way of their friendship. Jesus acts to abolish any sense of inequality that exists because of their social roles. Sandra Schneiders notes:

But any act of service is permissible and freeing among friends. By washing his disciples' feet Jesus overcame by love the inequality that existed by nature between himself and those whom he had chosen as friends. He established an intimacy with them that superseded his superiority and signaled their access to everything that he had received from his Father (see [John]15:15), even to the glory he had been given as Son (see [John]17:22).[4]

Jesus exemplifies someone who, out of great love and with genuine affection, offers a gesture of tenderness and care that we can come to expect from our friends. He delights in serving, puts their needs ahead of his own and promises to share with his followers everything that he has been given. Jesus follows this up by saying, "You also ought to wash one another's feet" (John 13:14). He provides the apostles and all Christians an example to follow. This is how we are to be friends—by washing one another's feet. Friendship is messy, it takes time and it is a lot of work. The more we get to know someone, we soon discover our friends have obvious faults and annoying idiosyncrasies (don't we all?). Can we accept our friends for who they are, with all their beauty and their brokenness? Friendships are strengthened by our ability to put our friends' needs ahead of our own, and by allowing ourselves to be vulnerable in letting others take care of us when we are down. When we let go of our differences and inequalities, what remains is the genuine love of friends.

Experiencing God's Friendship

God wants to be friends with us. God so deeply wants to receive our friendship that God dared to become one of us through the person of Jesus. Do I believe that God wants to be friends with me? How does friendship with God happen? How do our face-to-face friendships give us an avenue to experience friendship with God?

Most friendships begin with some kind of shared experience. Where have you experienced God's presence? We meet God in surprising places. Perhaps you see God in the stunning natural beauty of a colorful sunset or a shooting star against a dark sky. Do you hear God through the magnificent sounds of the opera or an evening at the symphony? I have friends who recently welcomed their first child. They are overwhelmed daily by this miracle of new life and the countless ways they see God at work as they watch their baby grow. Maybe you have encountered God during a visit to a holy site, a favorite church, or while on pilgrimage to a sacred place.

Friendships are strengthened when we intentionally spend time with our friends. When was the last time you intentionally shared time with God? It is important that we spend time together, just for the sake of the relationship. One way to do this is through prayer. Spend some time with God. Talk with him about your day and tell him what's really on your mind. If you have any hesitations about this friendship—let God know and ask God to respond to your concerns. You may also want to revisit the chapter on prayer for more ideas on building a relationship with God through prayer.

As we discover this relationship with God, do we allow God to love us in return? A friend of mine likes to say, "God is absolutely crazy about you, like a teenager, giddy in love!" Think about those silly infatuated moments that teenagers share together. Do we allow ourselves to creatively waste time together with God doing nothing? Just staring at each other? When I was a giddy teenager, I had a huge crush on a boy who lived down the street. I used to walk by his house every day on the off chance that he would look out the window and see me passing by. This is how God loves us. God does this for us every single day! God comes walking by the places where we spend time, hoping that we will look up and catch a glimpse, and notice God standing right there.

Like a good friend, God knows us so well. God loves all of us equally, and God knows each one of us uniquely. God knows the things that give us great joy and delight. God knows the people who we need to come into our path that will help form us and shape us. God knows the situations that we need for growth. God knows when a glimmer of sunshine will brighten our day. God is constantly working on our behalf. Ask yourself, "How is God showing this great love for me in this very moment?"

Our face-to-face friendships are another way in which we can experience God's abiding presence and deep love. Several years ago, I was shocked to learn of the sudden death of a classmate. Sarah was one of the first people I met when I started graduate school. She was a constant presence in the dining hall, library and around campus. People were easily drawn in by her bright smile and gentle laugh. There is an empty space left in her absence; it is still so hard to comprehend that she is gone. As students and faculty gathered for Sarah's memorial service, I found comfort in Scripture, songs, friends and strangers alike. I was particularly grateful for the presence of a favorite professor. I assumed that she had been Sarah's advisor or teacher. When I inquired, she said that she never knew Sarah. She said, "I'm here because you're here." I was touched by her care and concern for the group of students who gathered to mourn the loss of our friend.

Afterward, several of us went out to eat at this little Thai noodle shop, where surely all of us had shared a meal with Sarah at one point. We retold our favorite stories about Sarah, and expressed words of appreciation for one another's friendships. How lucky we are to have known her! She taught us so much, and she was so full of life. The death of someone so young is a powerful reminder that life is short, and it serves as a reminder to tell those who mean the most to us that we love them. Our lives are forever different because of Sarah's life and now her death.

There were many tears shed that day, but surrounded by good friends, I knew God's love in a profound and absolute way. We experienced the peace that comes from being in God's presence. Jesus says, "For where two or three are gathered in my name, I am there among them" (Matthew 18:20). The words of Scripture seemed to be perfectly chosen to comfort our sorrow. The presence of a beloved teacher spoke volumes about her concern for our academic and spiritual lives. We were nourished by the Eucharist we shared and the meal we enjoyed together. Most profoundly, God was present in family and friends who joined together with a common faith to celebrate Sarah's life and entrust her soul into the loving arms of God.

Community is an important place where we experience the presence of God. Our friendship with God is not only a personal relationship, but it is a relationship that continues, grows and bears fruit in our relationship with the wider community of faith. This might happen within a church community or within friendships that exist in a spiritual setting (like a Bible study or faith-sharing group). Many women have strong relationships with other women that can lead to spiritual friendships whether that is a group of young moms in a playgroup or volunteers who share Christian values. Friends who are able to share faith openly are rare. When we find them, they are a real gift and provide tremendous support for one another.

As friends and followers of Jesus, we are the body of Christ in the world today. We become the presence of Christ for one another when our friendships embody the relationship we have with God. In friendship we are given the chance to know someone and be known by them, to see others at their best and worst, and to love them anyway. God unconditionally loves us in this same way. Friendship is a place where we forgive and are forgiven just as God forgives our faults and failings. The bonds of friendship are strengthened through the generous giving of ourselves and washing each other's feet. When we intentionally share all that God has given us with our friends, we become the face of Christ for others. And it is through the face of friendship that we come to see the face of Christ.

FOOD FOR THOUGHT

1. Think of one of your close friends. What are some qualities that you most appreciate about your friendship with this person? How did you become friends and why do you choose to remain friends?

2. How has technology enhanced your friendships? Has technology ever gotten in the way of communicating with your friends? Check out the Called to Holiness Web site (www.CalledToHoliness.org) or search for the "Called to Holiness" or "Finding My Voice" groups on Facebook. Post your own questions or reflections about friendship with others and friendship with God.

3. Are there friends who have come and gone in your life? Was there a noticeable break in the friendship or did you slowly drift apart? How does this friendship continue to impact your life? Spend some time journaling or writing a letter to this person expressing your gratitude for their friendship.

4. What has your journey of friendship with Jesus been like? When have you experienced Jesus' friendship most closely? What do you struggle with? What has gotten in the way? Spend some time talking with Jesus about your hopes and dreams for this friendship.

RITUAL

If you are reading this book within a small group setting, consider celebrating your friendship by washing each other's feet. You will need a large bowl, a pitcher of warm water and a small towel. Have one person seated in a chair while another kneels on the floor. As you take turns washing each other's feet, the person washing may want to share a brief memory or prayer for the person whose feet are being washed. Here are some examples:

I am grateful for our friendship because

I remember the time when we

_____

I am sorry for the time when

_____

My greatest hope for you is

_____

I pray that you

_____

I hope we continue as friends so that

_____

CLOSING PRAYER

Loving God, you bless us with the gift of friendship.
We give you thanks for these our friends.
Help us to share our lives more intimately and know each
    other more closely.
Through this washing of feet, may we come to know your love
    and care for each of us.
May we be drawn to serve others and share your friendship
    with all those we meet.
Amen.

CHAPTER FIVE

• SEX IN THE CITY OF GOD: THE
SPIRITUALITY OF SEXUALITY •

Nothing is more practical than finding God,
    that is, than falling in love in a quite absolute, final way.
What you are in love with, what seizes your imagination,
    will affect everything.
It will decide what will get you out of the bed in the morning,
    what you do with your evenings, how you spend your week-
        ends,
    what you read, who you know, what breaks your heart,
    what amazes you with joy and gratitude.
Fall in love, stay in love,
    and it will decide everything.
                —*Fall in Love*, a prayer attributed to Pedro Arrupe, S.J. [1]

"What happens in New York stays in New York!" This was the promise Meredith and I made to one another as we hopped a plane to the
Big Apple for a girl's weekend away. Like the girlfriends from the popular movie and television series *Sex and the City*, Meredith and I
explored the city sharing countless funny, awkward and intimate conversations about dating, sex and being single. To this day, when either
of us mentions "that one restaurant in New York," we immediately

begin blushing and break into a fit of giggles as we recall a dinner conversation filled with embarrassing innuendos.

Unfortunately, the topic of sexuality is often treated much like the promise Meredith and I made on the airplane. We don't like to talk about it in polite company. While growing up, I never talked to my parents about sex. I didn't talk to them about dating or boyfriends or anything related to the human reproduction system. The fact that there is an entire chapter in this book dedicated to the spirituality of sexuality (and presumably, my mother is going to read this!) makes me a little uneasy. Talking about sexuality can be complicated, and it makes us nervous—even for healthy, well-formed adults.

Many of us grew up with negative messages that sex is dirty, something to be avoided, or something that invokes feelings of guilt or fear. If the sex talk that you got from your parents was anything like mine, I learned that there are a lot of *NOs* when it comes to sex. My parents' list read much like the Ten Commandments—a string of rules each beginning with "thou shalt not" on every subject from pre-marital sex to birth control to abortion. Looking back, I probably received the best sex education in biology class, followed by conversations in the girl's locker room, and mostly from reading *Seventeen* magazine.

Even at my Catholic high school, when the topic of sexuality was raised in religion class, it was presented as an irrevocable list of rules. While parents and teachers offered many good reasons to avoid intercourse outside the context of a loving, committed marriage, their explanations provoked a lot of fear. I was afraid of getting pregnant, afraid of contracting a sexually transmitted disease, afraid of what people would think of me if I got caught kissing my boyfriend—and to be perfectly honest, afraid to talk with anyone about any of these subjects.

On the other hand, I know women for whom sexuality presents no fear whatsoever. There is a prevailing attitude that safe sex is OK as long as nobody gets hurt. Casual relationships are common in our hookup culture, where anything goes—from kissing to intimate touching to getting between the sheets—without ever establishing a real commitment. Even our language has a tendency to diminish the significance of sexual experiences. People say, "It's no big deal. We're just having sex." While it is important to feel confident in our bodies and self-assured in our relationships, sexuality is not something to be taken lightly. Sexuality is beautiful, powerful, awesome and mysterious. We might laugh at the occasional crude joke or flippant comment, but I think most people would agree that talking about sex requires some discretion.

Sexuality is a conversation that is long overdue. In my work with college students, I've had endless late-night discussions with women in serious dating relationships, wondering if they're ready to take the next step. I know young adults who are perfectly comfortable having "safe sex" but still feel like something is missing from their relationships. I wonder about a friend who is juggling a full-time job, a mortgage and a marriage; and she's concerned that having kids will only complicate her already busy life. I have several friends who have faced infertility issues, and I recently met a mom preparing to have "the talk" with her preteen daughter. I often think about a girl I met many years ago, who painfully recalled the unwanted sexual advances imposed upon her by a teacher and the long journey she endured toward regaining trust and learning to love again.

There is not space in this chapter to say everything, but it is a conversation we cannot ignore. Even as I sat down to write this, I found myself navigating a myriad of voices. For a subject that we often don't like to talk about, it seems that everyone has an opinion, including parents, friends and politicians. Not to mention the voice of a significant other, the body's voice, our desire for physical intimacy and the still small voice that lies deep within our conscience.

When it comes to sexuality, perhaps the voice that has both failed miserably and is most often misunderstood is the voice of the church. Young adults today raise many valid issues and objections to the church's teaching on sexuality. Some say that the church's teaching on sexuality is irrelevant and out of touch with today's generation. In the wake of the clergy sex abuse scandal, many say that the church has lost its authoritative voice.

Until the church thoughtfully acknowledges the experience of young adults—and its own missteps—it will not be seen as a legitimate authority in matters of sexuality. Young adults need a forum to explore their questions about sex and the church's teaching to help them develop healthy, integrated lives. By embracing this challenge, the church can become a safer, healthier and holier place for young people where leaders speak with a compassionate voice.

At the heart of the church's teaching on sexuality is a resounding "yes" to transformative and life-giving love, a love that is modeled by God's love for us. God's love is infinite and unconditional. It sees beyond race, gender, country of origin, sexual orientation, physical ability or intellectual capacity. Our Christian tradition teaches us that all of life is sacred. Each one is precious in God's eyes. Every life is deserving of dignity, respect and the opportunity to rise to his or her fullest potential. A well-developed understanding of sexuality moves us beyond our own self interests and opens our eyes to the needs and concerns of others.

My hope is for young adults to embrace a healthy and holy vision of sexuality based in selfless love. This may seem countercultural, especially in a society that has reduced sex to physical pleasure alone. In some ways, it even challenges the church's teaching on sexuality, which is too often articulated only in terms of procreation and marriage. What young adults need today is a healthy and holy understanding of sexuality that promotes loving and life-giving relationships. Instead of a "just say no" attitude toward sex, we need to say a resounding "yes" to love.

Let's Talk About Sex

Maybe the best place to begin is by clarifying some terminology. Sex and sexuality are two words which are similar but not necessarily interchangeable. While *sex* is used to refer to one's gender, we also use the word *sex* to mean genital intercourse. Sexuality, on the other hand, is something deeper and much more complex. Sexuality is about our underlying desires and passion.

Sexuality is bigger than sex. Sexuality is that inherent desire to connect with others, to create with others and to share life with others. Genital sex is only one expression of that. Sexuality encompasses values, feelings, behaviors, attitudes, self-knowledge and intimacy. Sexuality includes a person's capacity for love, compassion and vulnerability. It is much broader than one's gender or any one physical encounter. While *sex* is what we do with our bodies, *sexuality* is how we make sense of that experience. It is a way of being in the world, interacting with ourselves and with others.

Just as there is a lot more to sex than sexual intercourse, there is much more to sexuality than physical intimacy. Sexuality encompasses the hormonal feelings and physical changes that accompany adolescence to the innate desire to be close to others in a physical or emotional way. Sexuality is a gift that God gives to us. There is an inherent desire within each of us to create new life, to love and to be with others. It expresses itself in many different ways, but the source of that desire is our sexuality which comes from God. Sexuality is not simply about who I am dating, but how I am making God's love known in the world.

In his book *The Holy Longing* Ronald Rolheiser says,

> Sexuality is not simply about finding a lover or even finding a friend. It is about overcoming separateness by giving life and blessing it. Thus in its maturity, sexuality is about giving oneself over to community, friendship, family, service, creativity, humor, delight, and martyrdom so that, with God, we can help bring life into the world.[2]

One of the best euphemisms that we have for sex is "making love." 1 John reminds us that our ability to love comes from God. "We love because he first loved us" (1 John 4:19). Sexuality at its best binds us together and connects us to the source of love and life itself—which is God. Sexuality used well is life-giving and makes love present in the world. All of us have the ability to share God's love with others and bring life into the world. How do you show love? How do you create love? How do you *make* love?

Genuine love opens the possibility of bringing new life into the world. New life abounds when we use our creative energies to give birth, make lives whole and bring people together. New life expresses itself through friendship, teaching, mentoring, child birth, adoption, visiting a sick friend in the hospital, bringing joy to people through the gift of music, welcoming guests into your home, creating works of art, or time spent in prayer. Who are you in love with? And how is new life coming forth from that love?

Falling in Love: A Healthy Holy Love Life

In his book *My Life With the Saints*, Father James Martin reflects on the humor, kindness and affection shown by Pope John XXIII. He speaks candidly about the spiritual discipline of celibacy, and how love has manifested itself in his life through prayer, ministry and his relationships with family and friends. He even talks about his experience of falling in love.

Martin says that falling in love is one of the most wonderful parts of being human. It is perhaps the most human thing we could do. He asserts that all of us will fall in love at some point. As a loving person, you will naturally be attracted to others and they will be attracted to you. As a Jesuit novice, he was horrified at the thought of falling in love, and he shares the poignant advice he received from his novice director:

> If you hope to be a loving man or woman, you will inevitably run the "risk" of falling in love.... "If you don't fall in love...then there's something wrong with you." ..."It's human and it's natural. Loving is the most important part of being a Christian. The question is what do you do when you fall in love?"...what choices do you make and how do you respond?[3]

While few are called to celibacy, we are all called to relationships that are healthy and holy, that reverence one another in both mind and action. The virtue of chastity, the ability to give and receive love, is something toward which we can all strive. Chastity does not necessarily mean a complete renunciation of sex, rather it directs us toward the right use of sexuality in accordance with our state in life. Contrary to some perceptions, chastity does not imply that one is cold, heartless, or a prude. If anything, it frees a person to be loving, honest and warm. It is certainly not a bad thing to be attracted to people! The spiritual challenge is to find ways to express that attraction in a way that is healthy and life-giving.

We express our affection for others through spoken and written words, through touch and by other physical signs. We also express ourselves through our actions. Exchanging gifts, spending time together and tending to a sick child all say something about our concern for the other and our level of commitment in the relationship. One way to measure healthy expressions of attraction might be to ask, "Are my words and actions consistent with my intentions? Do they adequately express my level of commitment in the relationship? Am I choosing words and selfless actions that foster and strengthen the relationship?" Healthy expressions of love, whether they are verbal, physical or active deeds should always enhance the life of the other person.

I received an e-mail recently from my college boyfriend. He is coming to Chicago for a conference and wants to get together for dinner. While our visit will be strictly as friends (he is now married), I will freely admit that my heart nearly jumped out of my chest when his name appeared in my e-mail account. I did not anticipate the adrenaline rush, but I trust that's a normal and healthy response to what was once a fun, romantic and enjoyable relationship. He and I always enjoy reminiscing about our college days, but the authentic love we share as friends is one that honors the separate paths our lives have taken. We are able to be together in a way that reaffirms his commitment to marriage and respects my being single. I listen with admiration as he brags about his kids, he asks about my latest travels and our fondness for one another is conveyed with a warm embrace.

Ultimately, in any relationship, genuine love leads to greater freedom. Freedom in love allows a person to let go of self-interest and invites mutual respect rather than coercion, jealousy or self-centered decisions. Freedom leads us to a place where we are no longer caught up in what our egos want, need or desire from the relationship. Rather it allows us to keep the best interests of the other person in mind. Likewise, I am more willing to listen, consider another person's opinion, make compromises, and change because I trust that the one who loves me has my best interests at heart. I should not feel trapped or somehow limited in my potential. True freedom is the ability to give and receive love in trust, and is done in a way that leads both people to wholeness.

Intimacy and Nakedness

We all need to be loved. Companionship with roommates, sorority sisters, coworkers, a boyfriend or a spouse can bring us great happiness and fulfillment. But it is not uncommon to feel uncertain, lonely or confused when day-to-day relationships leave us desiring something more. Do you ever feel like all your girlfriends are engaged or married, and you're convinced that you are to be "forever a bridesmaid and never a bride"? Do you find yourself stuck in a job or confronted by an overpowering boss? At some point all newlyweds are confronted with each other's bad habits alongside their partner's best qualities. Those who move far from home struggle to keep in touch with family members and old friends. Have you ever mustered up the courage to break off a bad relationship, only to find yourself spending Saturday night at home? In these moments, it is only natural that we begin to crave security and solidarity with someone else who understands what we're going through.

What so many young adults are looking for today is an experience of intimacy. The desire to be known, the need to be understood at an emotional level and the craving for physical affection is all part of being human. I sometimes think that young adults today are so programmed for instant results and immediate gratification, that we lack the patience needed to establish a real, lasting and profound connection with others. It is not uncommon to confuse our need for intimacy with a desire for physical affection. Popular culture has convinced us that what we want is sex, when what we really long for is a loving relationship.

Intimacy is the ability to be "up close" with people. In intimacy there is an emotional and moral presence, even when the other person isn't physically present. My actions, decisions and desires continue to be guided and influenced by this other person even when he or she is far away. Intimacy involves being close to another person and still maintaining an authentic sense of self. Intimacy has been described as "proximity that liberates." Who do you stand next to and find yourself with a greater sense of freedom? When you are in their presence are you more yourself? Intimacy promotes a spirit of hospitality and openness where both people can risk being their true selves.

Ongoing intimacy requires ongoing presence with another. It takes real commitment and fidelity. Intimacy is sustained through the mundane moments of life, it is celebrated with every anniversary and it is strengthened during times of adversity. Intimacy results from shared experiences that draw us closer together—laughing at each other's jokes, listening to his favorite music, accepting an honest and fair critique of my work, wrestling with balancing work and life, negotiating about parenting styles and relaxing in the shared silence of each other's company.

Intimacy means I don't have to put on a pretty face every day. It means I can be angry, you can have a migraine and we can disagree. Intimacy requires that we allow for flexibility, make compromises, admit our mistakes, accept each other's faults and be ready to forgive.

Real intimacy requires that we get *naked* with each other. To stand naked in front of someone is to say, "This is who I am." It says that I trust you are going to love me just the same, if not more when you see what is hidden beneath my clothes. We were born naked. It is the most natural state of being. Lovers choose to be naked with each other. Being naked is the place of ultimate vulnerability. Getting naked in front of someone says that you're willing to expose *everything* both physically and emotionally.

Nakedness says, "I'm willing to let you see my flaws." I'm willing to let you see my imperfections, my deficiencies and my faults. True lovers don't care if there is a scar, a mole, a roll of fat, a missing arm or breast or other imperfections. It says that I'm prepared to see the other person's flaws and accept that person in the same way. When we love another, we embrace them with a full heart—flaws included.

Nakedness says, "Let me show you my scars." Let me show you those places where I've been hurt and injured, and let me show you where I've found healing. I want you to see the place where I sliced my leg on a piece of barbed wire when I was nine, and I want to share with you the lessons I learned from the last painful breakup. I have scars left over from a skinned knee, a bruised ego and a broken heart. I want you to see the humility, strength and determination that it took to mend them back together.

Nakedness says, "I'm willing to let you touch the most private parts of my life." I want to take you to the places where no one else gets to go, and show you the things that nobody else gets to see. It is the place of ultimate vulnerability. I want you to understand my past resentments, share in my dreams for the future and hold me through tears of joy, sorrow, sickness or grief.

True lovers are prepared to get naked with one another. Until you're ready to love all of me, as a human body with all its curves and crevices, and as a human being with all my flaws, scars and private parts, then I'm not sure we should be getting naked.

Sexuality at its best results from genuine intimacy. A real relationship requires intimacy that goes beyond what happens in the bedroom.

Richard Malloy reminds us that people can enjoy deep intimacy without having sex. He says:

> Sex without a real, intimate connection may be a pleasant experience, but it ultimately fails. Sex is more than sex, it is designed to make us go beyond ourselves to become who and what we truly desire to be, that which we are created to be: lovers. Opening yourself and disciplining yourself to achieve and receive the grace of intimacy is a much more soul satisfying way to live your life.[4]

Ungraceful Experimentation

Sexual sin is often thought of as the worst kind of sin but, of course, this is not because sex is sinful in itself. Sinfulness involves actions, attitudes and behaviors that separate us from God's love. Because sexuality has the potential to enhance a close, loving relationship with another human being, it must be treated with care. Wrongful use of sex often goes hand-in-hand with wrongful use of another person—the crux of the sin. Sexual feelings, in and of themselves, are not sinful. It is what we do with them, how we respond to them and the ways we choose to integrate sexuality into our lives that either lead us closer to God or away from God, closer to the person we love, or further away.

As we journey from adolescence into adulthood, from curious teenagers to caring adults, we gradually move into a greater awareness of sexual maturity. Our efforts toward integration are a continual process, and God's grace is constantly at work in us. We do not learn how to be intimate, affectionate, vulnerable, honest, communicative and committed in a single day. It takes a lifetime of relationships and experiences to understand ourselves as sexual beings. And it does not happen without the occasional mistake or misunderstanding.

Sexual experimentation at a young age can be especially awkward and ungraceful. Many of us remember being that adolescent girl growing into her body, adjusting to the way hormones fluctuate, and perhaps overcoming social awkwardness. Through exploration and experimentation we came to know our bodies and grew comfortable with our ever-changing physical selves. We learned what felt good and what felt strange, and we learned to express ourselves within a loving relationship. Physical expressions of love are appropriate to the extent that the touching is proportional to the level of commitment. Setting boundaries is important, and yet sometimes we don't discover where the boundaries need to be set until they have already been crossed.

I've certainly had my fair share of ungraceful moments. While I am not always proud of the choices I've made in my relationships, the ungraceful moments have taught me a lot about what I was looking for in a truly loving relationship. Maybe you recognize yourself or those around you in some of these ungraceful moments, too. Perhaps you have been used by someone for their sexual pleasure or you have taken advantage of someone else. You have been hurt by ignorance, immaturity or fear—your own or someone else's. You know the guilt of going too far, even when your conscience told you to be careful. Your judgment has been impaired after a night on the town, and you would have made a different decision had you been sober. You find yourself saying "we should really stop," but your body language gives every indication that you want to keep going. You follow what feels good without any regard for the other person's physical or emotional well-being (or your own).

Perhaps one of the most ungraceful moments for college students is the "walk of shame." The phrase itself elicits the humiliation and guilt experienced by a student who finds herself walking back to her dorm early in the morning, after spending the night with a guy she barely knows, wearing the same clothes she had on the night before, and hoping no one notices.

Shame and guilt are complex emotions. Healthy shame monitors closeness and separateness. It alerts us to boundaries, guides our discretion and builds a sense of personal dignity. Likewise, guilt monitors our sense of belonging, and it measures correctness of our actions. A healthy sense of shame or guilt can be a good thing. Looking back on the past can be painful, especially when we know we've messed up, and it's even more difficult when we've been hurt by someone else. It may feel like your life is ruined forever, but living in a constant state of regret will only lead to despair. An unhealthy sense of remorse, believing that I am no longer lovable or not worthy of forgiveness, creates a downward spiral away from God.

Knowing God's complete and unconditional love is central to trusting in God's unfailing mercy. When we acknowledge our poor choices or imperfect judgment, our guilty feelings invite us into genuine sorrow. We learn that God's love is always available. God knows our best intentions and gives us the freedom to choose right from wrong. Even when that bond of trust is broken, forgiveness is extended. We have only to say, "I'm sorry." Forgiveness gives us the grace we need to start over and the energy to risk loving again.

God is not waiting to pounce on our every mistake. But it is important to be honest about our past experiences, their effect on us, and the impact they have on others. In this way, incidents that leave us feeling vulnerable also open us to God's care and concern for us. When we reflect on them in a safe space—through journal writing, a conversation with a trusted friend, in reconciliation or spiritual direction—we begin to recognize God's grace in those moments. We can let go of our mistakes and move on with our lives. The ability to be self-reflective also helps us to become more other-centered. It helps us understand our own motivations, see the other person's point of view, and make decisions that are best for everyone involved. Admitting our mistakes and accepting forgiveness is all part of the process as we move toward authentic love.

Selfless Love

As we grow in sexual maturity, how can we best respond to God's invitation to loving relationships in ways that are healthy and holy? What does that look like? One place to look is in the Scripture. There are so many wonderful examples of Jesus exhibiting healthy intimacy and selfless love.

Jesus welcomes women, men, children and strangers (Luke 19:1–10, 8:1–3; Mark 10:13–16, 7:24–30). Jesus eats, laughs, teaches and tells stories (Matthew 9:9–13; Luke 11:1–13, 15:1–32). He touches people (Mark 7:31–37, 8:22–25) and allows himself to be touched (Mark 14:3–9; Luke 8:43–48). Jesus mourns the loss of a friend (John 11:30–44), heals those who are sick (Matthew 9:18–25; Luke 13:10–17), and extends forgiveness to sinners (John 8:2–11). Jesus courageously confronts authority and challenges people's assumptions (Mark 12:13–17; Luke 6:27–36, 10:25–36).

Jesus shows us the way toward sexual integration—using our bodies and our lives to bear love, share intimacy, offer healing and bring life into the world. This kind of authentic love leads us closer to God and unites us with others. Sexual integration is not always easy. It is a process, and it takes a lot of work.

Authentic love requires more than just imitating what is popular. It means we must move beyond doing what simply feels good to what *is* good. There is a real temptation to boil our sexual ethics down to right-and-wrong answers. My parents' list of thou-shall-not commandments may have been suitable advice for a fourteen-year-old still developing an adult conscience and learning to comprehend the subtle nuances of a mature faith. Our conscience is the voice of God resounding from deep within, and a well-formed conscience is shaped over time. In order to say "yes" to what is truly loving, it takes practice, discipline, prayer, study and honest self-reflection. Appropriate conscience formation assumes that we are intrinsically good. Our conscience reveals deeper truth, and we have the ability and desire to discern and choose what is right.

We all face different questions, decisions and situations at various stages in life. If you are faced with a particular challenge, this short examination of conscience may provide some space for reflection.

1. **Know that you are loved.** God's love is everywhere and always available to us. Do I think of God during the day and talk to God in my own words? Am I confident that God has good things in store for me? Do I accept the love and concern shown to me by others?

2. **Understand your motivations.** God sees beyond outward appearances and looks into our hearts (1 Samuel 16:7). What are my underlying motivations? Am I acting out of fear or out of love? Is there a particular need that I am trying to fill (such as a need for security, intimacy, acceptance, physical affection, pleasing others)? Is it an authentic desire or a fleeting passion? What is the popular choice? What is the countercultural response?

3. **Name your fears.** There is no fear in love, but perfect love casts out fear (1 John 4:18). What am I afraid of? Am I concerned about what others will think or say? Am I afraid of getting hurt? What do I risk losing? What is at stake (my pride, time commitments, freedom, financial security, need for control)? Is fear holding me back from making a decision?

4. **Respect all people.** God is creator of all life, and every person is precious in God's eyes. What impact do my actions, attitudes, decisions or indecision have on others? Do I treat my own body with the reverence and respect it deserves? How is life and love coming forth from this decision? Am I sensitive to the needs of others?

5. **Pray boldly.** God knows our needs, and God desires what is best for each of us. Have I brought my concerns honestly and earnestly to prayer? Am I able to listen with an open heart? What do I need from God? What does God want from me? Does God have something better in mind that I've not yet considered?

6. **Be grateful.** God will not be outdone in generosity. Am I grateful for all that God has given me? Do I trust that there will always be enough? Am I withholding my gifts from others out of fear or greed? Do I willingly share what I have with others?

7. Accept forgiveness. God does not love us any less because of our past mistakes and missteps. Am I constantly rehashing past mistakes? Is there a lesson I can carry forward from the past? Have I sought reconciliation with those I've hurt? Am I able to forgive those who have injured or disappointed me? Have I forgiven myself?

8. Discern wisely. God is the source of all wisdom. Am I trying to learn more about God through Scripture, education classes, or spiritual reading? Am I willing to look at an issue from multiple perspectives? Do I know the people and resources that are available, and do I seek their help? Am I willing to wait patiently for clarity? Do I jump to conclusions or make impulsive decisions? Do I listen and trust the voice that resounds deep within?

When we live out our sexuality with integrity, we are transformed into selfless people. The choices we make and decisions we face are not easy. Decision making, especially in the area of sexuality, is complex because our sexuality is woven so deeply into the fabric of our being. While our decisions are profoundly personal, they are also inherently interpersonal because we live in relationship with others. We must thoughtfully listen to the voices of those around us, but a well-formed conscience ultimately compels us to discern and trust the voice of God. As we mature in faith, we more readily respond in love.

Our sexuality is a natural part of who God made us to be. God's love is made visible and new life is possible when we understand ourselves as sexual beings. We are people who instinctively desire to connect with others, to create life and share love. In our best moments, our sexuality answers the questions, "How am I creating new life? How am I making God's love present in the world?" Sexuality is about using our lives, our bodies and our whole selves to give voice to God's love. It takes shape in community, family, friendship, prayer and artistic endeavors. Love has many expressions, new life is created in many forms and mature sexuality draws us into selfless service to those around us. Ultimately, a healthy and holy sense of sexuality leads us closer to others and closer to God.

FOOD FOR THOUGHT

1. Who are you in love with? (Romantic relationships? Other relationships?) How do you express that inherent desire to connect with others and share life with others? How is new life coming forth from that relationship?

2. Where do you encounter messages about sexuality in popular culture? What do movies, music and magazines say about sexuality, and what do they lead you to believe? What are some countercultural ways to live versus popular messages to hook up and see sexuality in casual, trivial ways?

3. What are the largest obstacles to your having a healthy sexual relationship? From what do you need to be freed in the area of sexuality?

4. What are your deepest desires for yourself as a sexual person? What are your greatest hopes for being loved and loving others?

CHAPTER SIX

• Becoming a Voice of Peace in a Turbulent World •

May God bless you with
discomfort
at easy answers,
half-truths,
and superficial relationships,
so that you may live
deep within your heart.

May God bless you with
anger
at injustice, oppression,
and exploitation of peoples, so
that you may work for justice,
freedom and peace.

May God bless you with
tears
to shed for those who suffer
pain, rejection, hunger and
war, so that you may reach out
your hand to comfort them and to
turn their pain into joy.

And may God bless you with enough
foolishness

to believe that you can make a difference
in this world, so that
you can do what
others claim cannot be done.

—*A Franciscan Blessing*

One morning a young woman in her late twenties wandered into my office.
I could sense that she was apprehensive about whether she had come to
the right place. Her clothes, age and demeanor suggested that she was
not a student. Her name was Tina, and she said she needed to talk to
someone. She explained to me that she and her young son were in danger. She had been beaten by her husband thirty days prior and her free
stay at a battered women's shelter was about to expire. She needed
money for bus fare to take her son and herself to family, and safety, in
Tennessee.

I was not sure what to say or how to respond. I spent a long time listening to her story—where she grew up, how she found her way to
Chicago, why she married this man and how much joy she found in raising her son. The more we talked, the more I sensed her tremendous
strength and her determination to start over and to have a better life. We
were able to find some resources for Tina, and I never saw her again.

This is not a typical encounter for me in my ministry. But it reminds
me that every day women find themselves in distressing and desperate
situations. Every day women are abused, taken advantage of, denied
opportunities for decent work and degraded in their human dignity.
And every day ordinary women find themselves in a position to help
those in need.

In every part of this country, we see women, men and children who
lack basic needs like food, shelter, education, adequate healthcare and a
decent wage. Poverty often affects women (and their children) more
than men. People whose lives are at risk live all around us. We know

some of them by name. They are our relatives, neighbors, coworkers and friends. Many more are the nameless strangers whom we pass on the street. Living in a big city, it is not uncommon to see people begging for change, sleeping on park benches, asking for bus fare, or stowing their belongings under the highway overpass. Yet you do not have to live in a major metropolitan area to witness the struggles of humanity. Human suffering exists in midsize cities, small towns and rural areas. The elderly, the imprisoned, people with physical challenges, financial difficulties and emotional distress all struggle to live day to day.

Our love of God and love of neighbor go hand-in-hand. Our fundamental call as Christian disciples requires that we care for the least among us. Jesus says, "Truly I tell you, just as you did it to one of the least of these who are members of my family, you did it to me" (Matthew 25:40). Caring for those who are hungry, thirsty or without shelter is good gospel living. Our love of God compels us to become the presence of Christ in the world. Working on behalf of the poor and marginalized is fundamental to our identity as disciples of Jesus. Living a service-centered life is not only something we *do*; it is who we are.

For young adults, it is easy to get caught up in our hurried lives. Why make time to do something "extra" for someone else? High school and college students are often advised that service hours look good on a résumé. One of the dangers of "fulfilling service hours" is that our good works become another thing to check off our to-do lists. When service is done as an obligation instead of something done out of freedom, it quickly becomes a burden instead of a joy. Likewise, the warm fuzzy feelings that come from doing good eventually wear off. Deep down we want to make a difference, but serving others is not always convenient. It doesn't always feel good. One of my first volunteer tutoring assignments was destined for frustration, as I continued to show up every week despite the students' sporadic attendance. I began to ask, "Why am I here? Why stay committed?" Justice is about doing the truth in love. It is an intentional decision to do the right thing. We continue to serve others even when it doesn't feel good, but it continues to feel right. Our call to Christian discipleship and the common bond of humanity stretches us beyond our initial motivations. We feel a sense of kinship with those we serve; these are our brothers and sisters. Working for the common good of all people becomes its own reward.

Creating Justice for Others: Living a Life of Service

I grew up with great role models for service—parents, priests, religious sisters and a strong lay community. My parents nurtured a life of service in my brothers and sisters and me that was ingrained from a young age. We baked cookies for our elderly neighbors and participated in clean-up days at our parish. During my college years, service projects were no longer forced excursions, but an active choice to make the world a better place. I spent countless hours tutoring at a local high school. Upon graduation, I spent a year teaching at an inner city high school in Chicago. My life of service has been the exception rather than the rule, yet it is becoming a familiar path for many young adults.

Many young adults of this current generation have dedicated their lives to service—from a few hours a week to those who commit several years of their life as a volunteer. Service learning programs are becoming an integral part of the curriculum at many high schools and colleges, while post-graduate service programs provide volunteers in urban and rural areas both domestically and abroad. The call to service, justice and social change is strong among young adults. The Catholic Network of Volunteer Services (CNVS) provides support for several hundred lay mission and volunteer organizations. Together, these organizations enlist over ten thousand volunteers each year with nearly 70 percent of their long term volunteers ranging between ages 21–25.[1] CNVS supports Catholic organizations such as Amate House, Dominican Volunteers USA, Jesuit Volunteer Corp and Passionist Volunteers International. Meanwhile, there are many other private, faith-based and government funded program such as Covenant House, Peace Corps and Teach for America just to name a few.

Volunteers spend a year (or two) teaching at low-income schools, and serving as case workers at homeless shelters, soup kitchens and social service agencies. They work in the areas of legal aid, parish ministry, healthcare and immigration. Young adults have many motivations for serving. We or someone we know have benefited from the generosity of others, or we have witnessed the impact that unjust social systems have on others. Walking into a school with peeling paint, empty bookshelves and outdated computer equipment is all it takes to realize that every kid deserves the opportunity for a good education. We have a sense of gratitude for the gifts and blessings in our own lives which motivate us to share what we have with those in need. We have a strong desire to change the world—even if that means making a difference for one person.

While many have a strong desire to serve, many do not have time or resources to commit a full year to volunteer service. Service takes on many shapes and forms. Your commitment can be as little as an hour or two a week, and there are many opportunities for occasional volunteers. It might include volunteering at a soup kitchen, tutoring with a literacy program, or providing food and clothing for a local shelter. Our works of justice include community organizing, leadership development, board membership and educating communities about justice issues. Some individuals are called to witness more publicly through demonstrations or civil disobedience. Still others choose a lifestyle of solidarity with the poor by living low on the consumer chain, buying locally grown food and through their choice of work. Being an ethical consumer requires us to be attentive to how we make money as well as how we spend it.

When I was in the third grade, Sister Veronica made us memorize the corporal works of mercy. I still find this to be a helpful checklist of opportunities to help those in need: feed the hungry, give drink to the thirsty, clothe the naked, shelter the homeless, visit the sick, visit the imprisoned and bury the dead. Another helpful resource within the

Called to Holiness series is Joan Mueller's book *Living a Spirituality of Action*. Joan provides an inventory that you can use to match your gifts, skills and professional training with non-profit organizations in your area. She also offers helpful suggestions for material giving that provide the greatest benefit to those who are the recipients of our generosity.

There is a truism about service that says, "You will receive much more than you will ever give." I have found this to be an accurate statement— both in my work as a volunteer and in my experience leading. Through service, we discover insights about our own lives that we typically cannot see when we're caught up in the day-to-day grind. We uncover gifts and skills that we didn't realize we possessed. We learn things about other people, perhaps notice assumptions that are simply not true, or find ourselves surprised by how much we have in common. Scott London summarizes Robert Coles's long time work with volunteers and observations about the transformative nature of service. "He finds that the volunteers who are the most successful are those who genuinely like the people they meet, who quickly lose the sense that they are martyrs making a sacrifice, and most importantly, who realize that they are getting something in return."[2]

After graduating from college, I spent a year at Amate House, the Young Adult Volunteer Program for the Archdiocese of Chicago. I moved to Chicago with a passion for teaching and a strong desire to "save the world." It was an incredible experience filled with new friendships and personal growth. In many ways, my year of teaching was everything I expected of an inner city high school. Discipline was a constant problem, and I spent much of my time trying to keep the students quiet and focused. On the other hand, I was surprised to find many students who were bright and talented, and whose parents wanted nothing but the best for their kids. They defied all of the stereotypes I had about inner city youth.

Despite my dreams to become the teacher who overcame all obstacles and inspired every student to greatness, I did not save the world.

Overall, the student body did not have the determination, discipline or desire to succeed that I had hoped for them. But I learned so much from my teaching experience. I have a much greater appreciation for racial diversity and the richness of different traditions. There were many times when I wanted to throw in the towel, yet I learned the power of perseverance. And I truly came to enjoy the students with whom I worked. Much of what I still do today is about embracing different perspectives, persevering through difficulty and inspiring the best in people. I could not have learned these lessons without spending a year at Amate House.

The Jesuit Volunteer Corp coined the phrase "ruined for life" to describe the impact that a year of service has on young adults. In other words, you will be different. This experience *will* change you. Service transforms us and moves us to a new level of understanding. It changes the way we view others and how we see ourselves. Dedicated service work joins all of God's people in living, learning, and helping one another. When we engage in volunteerism, we not only do something *for* someone else (serve a meal, build a house), but we also walk *with* them on the journey through life. By journeying together we automatically receive something in return. This reciprocal giving and receiving happens more naturally when we begin to see one another as a collaborative "we." It is not all about "us" helping "them." It is about all of humanity existing as God's people together.

Transformation as a result of direct service causes us to ask, "How will I live differently because of this experience?" Service can help affirm a call to teaching, social service, parenthood or health care. We could discover gifts such as compassion, patience, leadership or fundraising. We might uncover passion for a particular issue like homelessness, youth advocacy or HIV/AIDS awareness. Young adults effectively use their skills in business, marketing, media or communications to focus attention on these issues. Others successfully transfer their zeal for justice to the legal profession or to promote integrity in the workplace.

I once asked a young woman preparing for a year of volunteer work, "Why do you serve?" She said, "Because it makes me feel more alive! I am more fully myself when I am serving others." Ideally, service takes us outside of ourselves. Life is no longer about me and my needs. It puts our own wants into greater perspective. My faded winter coat doesn't seem so old when I encounter a homeless woman layered with blankets. I appreciate the chance to go outside for a long run even more after spending the afternoon with my grandma who has arthritis in both her knees. Being with the poor, the underprivileged or the suffering allows me to surrender some of my own preoccupations. As we set aside our own concerns, what remains is a more authentic sense of self. What remains is that part of us that most closely resembles God.

As we become more other centered through service, we are transformed from people with generous hearts to people of deep conviction. The relationships we develop with the poor and disadvantaged compel us to speak up and step out and name the injustices we see. In a profound way, service can help us find our voice, as well as the strength and courage to be the voice for others. We become the voice of those who have been silenced or who are not heard. We have the power to give voice to the atrocities that plague our world. We become the voice of peace and the voice of hope.

Living in a Violent World

Peace may seem an elusive goal for the twenty-first century. Where were you on September 11, 2001? Ask any young adult, and they will tell you the moment they first heard about the airplane strikes on the World Trade Center in New York City, the destruction at the Pentagon and the plane crash in rural Pennsylvania. We remember the moment the first pictures appeared online—the planes, the smoke, the building collapse and people scattering in every direction. There was the eerie sense of knowing that there would be few survivors, and we wept when we heard stories of 911 calls and cell phone messages sent from loved ones trapped on the highest floors above the point of impact. I was sitting at my desk finishing a conference call with a client when the news began to circulate through the office. As the severity of the situation sank in, I got that sinking feeling in the pit of my stomach. I began spinning through the Rolodex in my mind—who do I know in New York City? And are they OK?

We watched as the world stood still on September 11, 2001. The world was not a perfect place in 2001, but it was a time when young adults enjoyed a certain amount of prosperity. The 1990s were marked by the dotcom boom, a surplus of jobs and economic prosperity. Many of us had never really known a bad day in our nation's history. As one friend remarked, this is our generation's Pearl Harbor, our John F. Kennedy assassination, our Columbia space shuttle disaster multiplied a thousand times. Today, an entire generation seeks peace in an era marked by violence and postmarked by places like the Murrah Federal Building in Oklahoma City, Colorado's Columbine High School, the World Trade Center and Virginia Tech University—to name just a few.

Violence and suffering happen every day on a global scale. We can point to the war on terror in the Middle East, genocide in Darfur, civil unrest in countries like Rwanda and Iran, and the hunger and poverty that plague parts of Africa and Central America. Women around the world feel the impact of such violence in acute ways. Violence against women takes on a variety of forms. Domestic abuse is common in this country and others, where women suffer at the hands of boyfriends and husbands. Women lose their husbands and children to the tragedies of war, women themselves become innocent victims during combat and rape is still used as a weapon. In many countries, women are denied the opportunity for education. We hear stories of female genital mutilation, young girls forced to marry without their consent and women who are coerced into abortion out of a concern for family size or based on the gender of their unborn child. Unwanted babies are still left out to die in some parts of the world. All are violations of a woman's fundamental human rights.

It is sometimes easy to keep global violence and suffering at arm's length because the events are so far removed from our daily life. They happen in places where we have never been, to a people whose language we do not speak and within a culture we do not understand. But tragedies that happen overseas are as critical and significant as the violence that occurs in our schools and on our city streets.

I think it is possible to fail to see violence because it is so close. Violence has become so much a part of our everyday experience that we become numb to it. It is sometimes so close that we are blinded or even find ourselves justifying it. Violence happens to women we know; it happens to us. Women are victims of injustice, and sadly there are times when we perpetrate violence by our actions and our ignorance. The life and dignity of women is threatened every day. And we do not have to look far to see it.

Where Do You See Violence?

We summon violence with our eyes by what we watch and what we ignore. Violence is evoked through television, newspapers, videogames and magazines. Women are both subjected to, and objects of, this violence.

Pornography

I know a young woman who caught her boyfriend downloading pornographic photos from the Internet. He justified his actions by explaining that looking at pornography is like window shopping for a new car. "What harm is there in looking when you have no intention of buying?" In many ways, our society has made it acceptable for "boys to be boys." Watching sexually explicit movies, reading *Playboy* and going to strip clubs are sometimes encouraged as a rite of passage. The unhealthy sexualization in our culture and the objectification of women is harmful to both women and men.

Pornography dehumanizes women by diminishing them to sexual objects. It defines them by their bodies, and fails to see the whole of their lives. It erodes human dignity, denies authentic expressions of love and diminishes commitment within the relationship. True beauty is made into a spectacle or a sport.

Men are also victims of a violent culture. I once talked with a guy who viewed pornography on a regular basis. Despite having what seemed like a healthy relationship with his girlfriend, he could not seem to get out of this trap, and he struggled with a deep sense of regret and self-hatred. Pornography creates an illusion of intimacy without really being connected to the other person. The Internet makes it more accessible and leads to dangerous isolation.

Celebrity Obsession

There is an unhealthy obsession with celebrity in our culture. We look at women in magazines and movies, and we think their lives are perfect. For some strange reason, we think that because they have their names on a marquee or their photo on the front cover, they must have it all. We see something desirable in them—money, fame, beauty. We want to buy the labels they sport and wear the make-up they advertise. We imagine ourselves living that lifestyle. We are convinced that if we know their every move and every detail of their lives then perhaps we can someday become like them.

But obsession with celebrity turns us into slaves who hear and follow a drum beat that is not our own. It retards our ability to attend to and reverence our own stories—whatever they may be. We are sucked into the illusion. By constantly comparing ourselves to movie and pop stars we fail to see our unique beauty and goodness. Unhealthy idolizing of women's bodies by other women—whether via a celebrity obsession or the barrage of fashion magazines—creates a shallow and even erroneous understanding of beauty. How often have we heard that beauty is in the eye of the beholder, or that our all-important inner beauty is reflected in outer beauty in as many ways as there are people? Christian spirituality calls us to live deeply the truth that we are made in God's image—all of us—no matter what our genetic history, our physical appearance or our mental endowments.

Body Image

There are still other ways we commit violence to ourselves. I will be the first to admit that I love getting dressed up. I am all about pretty hair, high heels and a little black dress for a night out with friends. The cure-all for a bad week is to get my hair cut, and putting on a fresh coat of lipstick gives me energy to get through a long day. But how do we know when a legitimate desire to look nice becomes an obsession with body image? Instead of lifting us up, do we take revenge on ourselves with excessive use of food, drugs, alcohol or compulsive exercise? My friend "Angie" tells this story:

> No one asks for an eating disorder. It's not something that I ever felt that I consciously had control over. No one brings this on herself. When I was in grade school, despite have a loving family, good friends and many extracurricular activities, I experienced a lot of perceived emptiness in my life. I was convinced that I would never have the coolest friends, the right clothes or good enough grades. I began compulsively eating and binging primarily to "fill the void." Later, I was the girl who had everything—a good job, a beautiful condo, terrific friends and a great body. But on the inside, I was not happy. I was either not eating or compulsively overeating. It didn't matter how I looked in the mirror or the number on the scale—I felt fat and thought I looked ugly. The vicious cycle of overeating, binging, purging and over-exercising left me emotionally and physically exhausted.
>
> I was in my mid-twenties before I shared this with anyone. I was surprised to find many of my friends struggled, too. They know the self-critic that rattles in my mind. They know the lies that the mind sometimes tells us about our bodies. They've been there—afraid to look in the mirror, terrified of catching a glimpse of my reflection in a window and dreading the thought of swim-suit season. (Of course, here in sunny southern California every girl is expected to have a bikini-ready body for ten months out of the year!)

One of the most important things my friends taught me is that life is a journey filled with ups and downs and in-betweens. I don't have to be perfect all the time. These friends have become the voices of acceptance and solidarity; the voice of peace and shared pain. We have cried together, listened to one another's stories, and laughed together for hours on end. There are many days that I wish my eating disorder would just go away, but I've learned to accept this as a part of who I am. It is about progress not perfection; each day is a chance to start over again.

I think many women live with a perceived emptiness. It is easy to get caught up in what we do *not* have—a perfect body, the ideal relationship, the best job, a better house. There is a popular misperception that having the "perfect" body will create the perfect life. How easily we forget that we are already made in God's image and that true beauty comes from within, regardless of our shape and size.

Gratitude is a powerful spiritual tool and an effective antidote to perfectionism and self-criticism. God has given us so much! Being grateful for what I have (and not focusing on the things that I do not have) ensures that being present will be sufficient, that my possessions will suffice, and to trust what I give away will be returned in its own time. Gratitude opens us to the infinite capacity to love—including the ability to love ourselves. Every day give thanks to God for three things. Start small if you have to: I like my smile. I had a good conversation with a friend. I witnessed a random act of kindness from a stranger.

Addictive behaviors can also become unhealthy substitutes for situations and emotions that we would rather not face head-on. Adopting the virtues of honesty and truthfulness can free us from undue anxiety. Admit when you are happy, sad, angry, confused or scared; and develop the skills to deal directly with the situation at hand. Likewise, fear and worry tend to isolate us into our own little world. Let go of your need to go it alone. Reach out to friends and seek professional help if necessary. The more we are able to trust that God will provide for us, the less need we have for obsessive control over food, drink, people and circumstances.

We all want to be loved. We all want that "celebrity" attention. How easy it is to forget that God is absolutely crazy about you—just as you are! Alice Walker's award-winning novel *The Color Purple* chronicles the life of a poor black woman as told through her letters and diary entries. After a lifetime of abuse at the hands of her father and husband, Celie eventually breaks free with the love and help of her close friend Shug. In the following conversation we hear Shug telling Celie how much God loves the world and everything about us.

> Listen [Celie], God love everything you love—and a mess of stuff you don't. But more than anything else, God love admiration.
>
> You saying God vain? I ast.
>
> Naw, she say. Not vain, just wanting to share a good thing. I think it pisses God off if you walk by the color purple in a field somewhere and don't notice it.
>
> What it do when it pissed off? I ast.
>
> Oh, it make something else. People think pleasing God is all God care about. But any fool living in the world can see it always trying to please us back.
>
> Yeah? I say.
>
> Yeah, she say. It always making little surprises and springing them on us when us least expect.
>
> You mean it want to be loved, just like the Bible say.
>
> Yes, Celie, she say. Everything want to be loved. Us sing and dance, make faces and give flower bouquets, trying to be loved. You ever notice that trees do everything to git attention we do, except walk?[3]

It is Shug's example of genuine love and attention that helps Celie break free from a life of violence. We can counter violence against women by knowing, loving and celebrating the lives of women near and far. When we echo that divine love, we become the voice of God that affirms, admires and recognizes the contributions of women everywhere.

Where Do You Hear Violence?

Words are a powerful tool. The words that spew forth from our mouths have the power to create or to tear down. Words have the power to express love and to make war.

I was at a wedding last summer, where both the best man and maid of honor said some of the most horrible things about both the bride and the groom. The maid of honor implied that the bride married her fiancé for his law degree. The best man said the groom married his fiancée only to save her from her wretched mother. Everyone laughed. But there was an edge to the comments. I judged that it was not just good-natured humor, nor even the attempt to grandstand and be the center of attention. Do we know the difference between humor aimed ultimately at the good of others and humor that is intended to demean and cut down? There is a difference, and it is easy to overlook it or lose the knack of distinguishing between a genuine good laugh and destructive mocking. When one person is out to trump the other with a harsher jab, you can be sure that verbal violence is afoot.

The spiritual life involves a desire and commitment to truly listen to others and be aware of the things we say to one another. Do we appreciate each other's talents and encourage other women to succeed? The saying that "women are their own worst enemies" is sadly true in many settings. Who are we? People who undermine, undercut and devalue those within our family or circle of friends, or people who attend to the building up of the body of Christ and of the world, especially the world of women?

Gossip is a common and troublesome form of verbal violence. At what point does our genuine care and concern become idle talk about our friends and neighbors' personal matters? Maybe one friend is having a particularly difficult time; another is on the road to success; or there is a dispute between two friends and one seeks the advice of a third party. A simple reflection at the end of each day can help us discern whether gossip has gotten in the way of friendship. How do we talk about a friend when she is not in the room? Rule of thumb: Never say something that you wouldn't say if she were standing right in front of you.

Women can judge each other harshly. Women have fought for centuries to gain equal opportunity and acceptance. Yet, somehow when a friend or acquaintance uses her gifts and opportunities to be successful, we become jealous and judge her unjustly. We make assumptions about how she got where she is. We may accuse her of granting favors to get to the top; we may joke about her being hired as a "token woman" or as a statistic for equal opportunity employers rather than because she is smart and good at what she does. Do we understand why we feel compelled to cut her down? Do we have the spiritual resources to celebrate her success in our hearts, or at the least, express a word of congratulation?

The story of Martha and Mary from the Gospel of Luke (Luke 10:38–42) illustrates how such jealousy can lead to hurt feelings and judgment against one another. Martha, busy in the kitchen, is angry with her sister and insists that Jesus order her to help with the serving. Meanwhile, Mary is commended for sitting at the feet of Jesus. Martha is rebuked, not for her hard work, but as Jesus points out she is "worried and distracted by many things" (Luke 10:41). Martha is so concerned about the kitchen that she no longer takes joy in her work and does not appreciate her sister's choice to sit with Jesus. Furthermore, Jesus praises Mary for having "chosen the better part" (Luke 10:42)— focusing on the presence of God in her midst. Ideally, we develop a relationship with God through both our work and our prayer. We need to engage in both action and contemplation, and one need not come at the expense of the other. As women, do we judge one another for the choices we make? Does one woman's choice to stay at home or another's opportunity for career advancement leave her friends bitter and resentful? Remaining attentive to God's presence in our own lives helps us appreciate the actions and responsibilities of others, even when they are different from our own.

Women have had to work so hard to prove themselves in the workplace and yet stereotypes still exist: Strong women are labeled difficult, demanding and rigid; sensitive women are overemotional; women should not be taken seriously—even by other women. How often do we create a war of words with the things we say? Or create conflict in our minds to justify our own feelings of inadequacy? It is easy to become jealous and resentful of other women. At the same time, anger and jealousy tell us a lot about our own desires, dreams and hopes for the future. Perhaps we want the family, career, salary, prestige or attention that someone else has already achieved. If you find yourself in this situation, you may want to spend some time reflecting on what is underneath those strong emotions. What is really going on? Is my need to cast judgment on others an outward expression of fear, disappointment or impatience with myself?

At the end of each day, ask yourself, "Have I been a good friend and a supportive colleague to those around me?" Then ask God for the humility and courage to know how you contributed to any problems in your relationships. Find ways to incorporate gratitude and forgiveness into your daily life: Admit when you are wrong, acknowledge others when they are right, find genuine ways to say thank-you, apologize when necessary, give someone the benefit of the doubt if they're having a bad day, respect your own need for time alone or personal time with family and friends. We don't have to be best friends with every woman we meet. But working toward mutual understanding will nudge us closer toward becoming supportive colleagues and curbing unnecessary verbal violence.

Where Do You Touch Violence?

Not only do we see and hear violence into being, we can also create violence through touch. There are many ways that women are taken advantage of by others, and we sometimes unknowingly engage in violence to ourselves and others.

Sexual Assault

It is estimated that one in four women have been sexually assaulted. Incidents and statistics are under-reported because women feel that it was partly their fault, or because our justice system can make it very difficult to obtain a conviction. In addition, most sexual assaults do not fit the typical scenario of a violent rape perpetrated by a stranger. My friend "Lisa" recalls this story of an incident that happened to her over ten years ago. She still chokes back tears when she remembers it. I've heard her tell this story several times, and unfortunately it is a story that is all too familiar. She is not the first young woman to tell this story. It is a story that many women share.

> I don't know why this happened to me. I'm a smart girl with a great job. We were just going out to have a good time. I started dating this guy and he seemed really nice. He said all the right things, and I believed him. I felt safe, and I really thought this relationship was going somewhere. One night we went out to the movies and then back to his place. We had a few drinks…we actually had more than a few drinks. One thing led to another… I told him we should stop. He convinced me that we should keep going…I said no. He said he wouldn't hurt me…I knew he wouldn't hurt me, but I really wanted him to stop. I kept telling him that I didn't want to do this. I don't think he believed me…because he kept going.
>
> Afterward, I felt completely betrayed and violated. I was uncertain to what extent it was my fault, and I didn't know who to blame. We had both been drinking, but I told him to stop. I'm

sure I said no. I'm sure of it. Why didn't he stop? I felt so dirty and ashamed. It hurt in every fiber of my being. They say if it doesn't kill you it will make you stronger. I tried to put it out of my mind. But for years, I just wanted to die.

Sexual innuendoes, alcohol consumption, sexual exploration and casual experimentation can easily lead someplace you'd rather not go. All of these factors place a woman at increased risk of sexual assault. Whether intoxicated or not, a person has no right to take advantage. Date rape often turns into a "he said, she said" situation. Many assaults go unreported because women fear that they will not be believed. Sexual assault can be even more harrowing when a young woman is coerced into sex by a teacher, neighbor, relative or family friend.

Similarly, nothing is more detrimental to women's self-worth than the "hook-up culture." Whether "hooking up" means a really good make out session, with or without clothes, intercourse or not—it reduces our sexuality to physical pleasure alone. Being "friends with benefits" makes it easier to have sex than to have a real relationship. Authentic relationships require that we care about this person beyond what happens in the bedroom. There is a degree of intimacy and an emotional bond that is missing when two people simply hook up for the night. While hooking up can seem to be a lot of fun and physically satisfying, it also implies a temporary, non-committal, objectification of one another. Is that really what you want?

It is easy for us to say that other people are worthy of dignity, rights and respect. Are you not also worthy? Finding your voice means finding the strength to recognize your own self-worth and inherent value as a human being and not an object of someone else's satisfaction. Women are so accustomed to giving to others and putting others ahead of themselves, but do we insist upon the same treatment in return? Jesus calls us to "love your neighbor as yourself" (Matthew 22:39). How do *you* want to be loved? One way we express a genuine love of self is by insisting on our fundamental rights. It is not arrogant or self-centered to expect that others love us in a way that upholds our human dignity. We deserve respect from members of the opposite sex; we have a right to set and maintain boundaries in a relationship; and we have a right to communicate our needs and express affection in appropriate ways. It is about saying yes to healthy relationships, because you are worthy of it.

Prostitution and Sex Trafficking
One of the most popular romantic comedies of all time features the glamorous Julia Roberts and the oh-so-handsome Richard Gere. *Pretty Woman* is the story of Hollywood Boulevard prostitute Vivian Ward (Roberts) who is hired by wealthy business owner Edward Lewis (Gere) to be his escort for a week in Los Angeles. He showers her with new clothes and a lavish hotel room, they attend several business functions together and a budding romance ensues. The movie is complete with a fairy tale ending. *Pretty Woman* is a highly romanticized version of the real-life risky business of prostitution. In the end, it's not about the money. It's a modern-day love story where opposites attract and two wrongs make right. Their ability to bring out the best in one another is quite convincing, but it is also quite misleading.

The average woman who seeks a life on the street does not discover the same happily-ever-after ending. Most women find their way onto the street after escaping a life of violence, abuse or incest at home. The street becomes a place of survival and prostitution is their security. These women roam the streets not because they enjoy it, but because they can see no other way. Yes, many of them deliberately choose to have sex for money. But many of them cannot see beyond the immediacy of their situation. Pimps and johns control, manipulate and degrade women. With every trick they turn, women risk being raped, beaten and even killed. They are caught in vicious cycles of abuse, along with the lure of money, drugs and quick fixes. There is no easy way out.

Similarly, every day young girls are lured into this country (and many others) to be sold into prostitution. Girls and women are made into sex slaves at the hands of criminals. Statistics on human trafficking vary widely, but even the most conservative estimates are staggering. The U.S. Department of State estimates 800,000 people[4] are trafficked across national borders each year, while UNICEF reports that at least 300,000 children and adolescents are prostituted every year in the United States alone.[5]

The sex trade has become a huge global business where girls as young as five years old are kidnapped from their homes to be used as sex slaves. Sadly some are even sold by their own parents where the youngest victims, particularly virgins, prove to be the most valuable commodities. Girls who are coerced into sex slavery are promised well-paying jobs, continued education and support for their families. They are persuaded, usually by a paid recruiter, who scopes out victims then arranges for their travel and transportation. Not until they reach their final destination do these young girls discover that they have been deceived about the nature of their work. They live in brothels where they are on-call twenty-four hours a day, forced to perform sexual acts on demand, repeatedly raped by customers and receive no pay. Any chance to escape is both difficult and dangerous.

Prostitution and sex trafficking have a horrible, destructive influence on women's human dignity. Many have never known that they are entitled to respect and love—just because they are human beings, God's beloved creatures. There are also major economic dimensions to prostitution and sex trafficking. Pimps get rich and the poor suffer disproportionately. While a few women consciously make a choice to sell their bodies for sex and see it as a business like any other, most do not. For most others, prostitution seems like the only viable choice, and breaking away is a challenge.

What is lost in prostitution is a woman's sense of her own dignity. Restoring a woman's intrinsic value and self-worth is paramount to a successful life off the street. Survivors of prostitution usually develop a tremendous distrust of men. Those who escape prostitution must deal with the physical effects of abuse and overcome humiliation, fear and psychological harm. Women become the primary source of healing for each other. Programs for women escaping prostitution exist throughout the country; some have even been started by fellow survivors.

Women restore dignity by attending to other women in shelters, in their neighborhood, in literacy programs, through the arts and by being present to hear each other's stories. Nothing is more satisfying than women friends, with whom you can be honest, open, vulnerable and have some good laughs. There is a connection that women feel with other women that needs to be cultivated and treasured. Have you ever struck up a conversation with a strange woman and connected immediately, even though you will never see each other again? This happens in dressing rooms, on airplanes and in waiting rooms. Such random encounters can have a profound effect on us. As women we need to name and celebrate the solidarity we feel with other women.

Where Do You "Consume" Injustice?

As women, let us enter the public square to demand justice in the workplace, fair business practices and equal treatment of men and women. All people have a right to fair wages and a right to equal pay for equal work. The *New York Times* recently cited work by the Current Population Survey indicating that, even in 2009, women still earn seventy-seven cents for every dollar earned by men. This deficiency in pay ultimately means less food for her family, lower-quality education for her children and a more precarious lifestyle during her retirement. Closing the wage gap requires action on behalf of all women. Women can support one another in their workplaces and network with other women in similar industries to raise awareness and petition for fair pay across the board.

As informed consumers, women make choices every day—at the shopping mall and in the grocery store—that can lead to the greater dignity of women everywhere. Do I know the source of the items I buy? Is the fruit on my table picked by migrant workers who leave their families for weeks or months at a time to earn a living elsewhere? What are the factory conditions where our meat is processed or our canned goods packaged? Are my designer clothes made in a sweatshop where women (and young girls) work long hours for very little pay? Do the coffee growers receive a just wage in exchange for their harvest?

In addition, what impact does our consumer culture have on young adult women entering the workforce? Many young women are conflicted about their desire to have a family, and the call to use their education and gifts to enter a career. Some are led to believe that a college-educated woman is "wasting her education" by becoming a mom. At the same time, other young adult women depend on a well-paying job to pay off college loans. How do I know how to balance these needs and desires?

Sometimes it seems like all of our options are good choices. God gives us the freedom to follow our true calling in life, and God is with you no matter which option you choose. As we listen for that quiet nudge, we gradually discover the deepest desires of our hearts—those things that motivate, inspire and wow us. Discernment invites God into our decision making through prayer, active listening and intentionally responding in the direction God is calling you. Our genuine desires put us most closely in touch with who God wants us to be. They give us the courage to trust in God and stay committed to the call despite external demands or pressure to succeed.

Unfortunately, most women do not have the luxury of such choices. Single women, some with children, those who work for minimum wage and families who depend on two incomes in order to survive have little choice about working or not working. For them, staying at home is a choice they can only dream about. In order to support all women, we need to advocate for fair pay, family medical leave and flexible work schedules that promote the good of all families, especially for families without the financial means to move ahead without these benefits.

Praying Through Suffering

So, where do we go from here? A seemingly endless list of injustices can leave us exhausted and with heavy hearts. It is easy to become cynical or overwhelmed. At times we may find ourselves outraged at the world in which we live, infuriated at those who have hurt us, confused by a culture that has predisposed us to violent tendencies, and frustrated with ourselves for the mistakes we've made. Reading and writing about injustice makes me angry, and I often wonder about how to channel that anger into something positive.

In our spiritual practice of prayer, righteous anger is expressed as a lament. Prayers of lament cry out that life isn't fair! The lament Psalms are cries of complaint against the injustices imposed upon us, and they insist that God has an obligation to change things. Meanwhile, God is silent and seems to have forgotten us. We wonder if God really sees the poor and the oppressed in our midst. There is a dark and empty loneliness that leaves victims asking, "Am I the only one?" The torment of war, the effects of abuse and the sting of sarcasm carry on long after the hostility has ceased. Our prayers of lament cry out, "Where are you God?" and "Why has this unfairness been dealt upon us?"

> How long, O LORD? Will you forget me forever?
>   How long will you hide your face from me?
> How long must I bear pain in my soul,
>   and have sorrow in my heart all day long?
> How long shall my enemy be exalted over me?
> (Psalm 13:1–2)

Prayers of lament give voice to our anger and our pain, and they demand that our concerns be taken seriously. It is not a cry of self-pity, but a vigorous insistence that something is not right, and we will not stand for it any longer. Those who endure suffering demand that their despair be heard, because once the truth is acknowledged and their pain is received, things may begin to change. As women, we are called to reverently hold space for this hurt to be expressed. Oftentimes a lament is the first hint of hope for those who are suffering. The expression of pain is essential to prayer. By including our prayers of lament, we speak our anguish aloud to God, who shares in the pain and suffering of the world through Christ. There is no escaping the cross. We encounter the struggles of daily life in our volunteer efforts, we carry the burdens of those whom we accompany on the journey and we are crucified by the injustices that are committed against us. Suffering is not a cross that we place upon ourselves, rather the cross is the place where divine mercy and human suffering meet. God meets us in the emptiness of grief, the isolation of addiction and the pain of sexual assault. Suffering is not good in and of itself. But suffering with the belief that God will restore us to new life enables us to experience God's mercy more abundantly. The cross becomes a symbol of hope when we allow it to transform us.

One of the marks of a lament is a profession of faith, a prayer of confidence in God or words of praise. Giving way to lament moves those who suffer to go beyond denial and toward hope, it compels those who recognize suffering in the world to work for justice and the act of lamenting connects all of us to God. Hope is essential to the spiritual life. Hope is the abiding sense that life prevails even after death; that love conquers all hatred; and peace is ultimately stronger than war. Hope rests in the belief that God is somehow at work through our struggles. Psalm 13 which cries out, "How long oh Lord?" ends with these hopeful words of praise:

> But I trusted in your steadfast love;
>   my heart shall rejoice in your salvation.
> I will sing to the LORD,
>   because he has dealt bountifully with me.
> (Psalm 13:5–6)

The Psalmist speaks confidently as if God's help is already on its way. When faced with adversity in our own lives or in our pursuit of justice for others, the spiritual challenge is always to remain faithful in the call to serve others, confident that God is ever-present, and certain that we will not be left to face our struggles alone.

So many women are waiting for a day when all people will live in right relationship with one another. Peace is not the absence of violence. Peace in our day is to know the presence of God so profoundly that we allow God's love to permeate all the places where we see, hear, feel or encounter violence. It is to trust in the transformative power of service and the life-giving power of the cross.

We become the voice of peace when we speak out on behalf of the poor and the vulnerable; when we raise our voices to uphold the dignity of others; when we become a voice of justice for those who have no voice. We become the presence of peace when we reverently hold space for victims of discrimination, violence and tragedy; so that their stories may be heard, anger can be expressed and the seeds of hope and healing begin to sprout. I can use my voice to speak my mind and insist upon dignity for all women—including myself.

Food for Thought

1. Where do you encounter the poor and vulnerable in your neighborhood, city or local community? How have you engaged in service or volunteerism? What is one thing you learned from your experience? How are you different?

2. How have you been touched by violence? Where have you seen, heard, touched or experienced violence around you? In what ways are you called to speak out on behalf of someone else who has been injured?

3. What are some ways that you can be the presence of peace and reverently hold space for victims of injustice? Consider ways to include them in your individual or community prayers.

4. Write a lament psalm. Choose an issue of injustice against women or an incident of personal hurt. Allow yourself to cry out to God and demand that your concerns be heard. Use honest words and phrases that scream, gripe, mourn and complain. Tell God how you really feel. End by giving praise to God and expressing hopeful anticipation that things will change.

The young adult years are often characterized by questions of self-discovery. Who am I really? Where am I going? How will I make a difference? These are the perennial concerns of every young woman as she pursues a career, family, friendships and other interests. Today's young adult women are maturing in a diverse and pluralistic culture with ever increasing advancements in technology. At the same time, the world in which we live is plagued by violence, poverty and injustice. This next generation of "spiritual but not necessarily religious" seekers continues to search out a place to ask questions and wonder "why?" Perhaps the greatest question is, "Where is God in all of this?"

The spiritual life holds many insights into the search for identity, the relationship with God, self and others, and the events that shape the lives of young adult women. We discover our voices through our friendships, by discerning our vocation, and from understanding ourselves as sexual beings. Through the voice of prayer we join in friendship with God, we hear Jesus calling us by name and we listen for the still small voice of the Holy Spirit. We use our voices to express righteous anger in the face of injustice, to demand dignity for all people and to become an expression of counterculturalism in a consumer-driven society.

We find our voices by listening to the stories of women and men who have gone before us marked with the sign of faith. There are so many who have crossed the threshold of young adulthood; women who found their voices as young adults and spent their lives in tireless pursuit of the gospel! The voices of women are hidden in the countless named and unnamed women in Scripture who ministered with Jesus and helped to found the early church. I think about the great women theologians of our time and the early Christian mystics whose extensive letters and writings give voice to their intimate experiences of God. There are many women who grace us with their presence every day—grandmothers, godmothers, aunts, moms, daughters, sisters, mentors and friends—who mirror God's presence and model God's love for us.

Dorothy Day

I think about Dorothy Day, founder of the Catholic Worker movement, who worked tirelessly on behalf of the poor. Dorothy spent many years resisting and questioning the call to faith. After her conversion to Catholicism, she became steadfast in her dedication to prayer and devotion to the Eucharist. A journalist by profession, the *Catholic Worker* was started as a newspaper used to publicize Catholic social teaching, and soon they began to open houses of hospitality for the homeless and destitute. Known for her radical social values, outspoken pacifist stance against war and profound yearning for the sacred, Dorothy Day became one of the strongest voices of peace and justice for the twentieth century.

Sister Thea Bowman

Sister Thea Bowman was a beloved preacher and teacher with a gift for proclaiming the Word of God. Thea did not write so much as she spoke and sang the gospel. By educating all people on the black religious, historical and cultural experience, Thea helped many people bring together their African American heritage and Catholic faith. One of her most notable public appearances came during a meeting of the U.S. Catholic Bishops in 1989 where she was invited to speak on the black Catholic experience. At the end of the meeting, Thea invited the bishops to stand and join hands, and they joined her in an emotional rendition of the African-American spiritual "We Shall Overcome." Sister Thea Bowman spent her life fighting prejudice, breaking down racial and cultural barriers and bringing people together through the gift of song, dance and the love of Jesus Christ.

Mary, Mother of God

Mary is often referred to as the first disciple. She was the first to recognize that the child she carried in her womb was the Savior. At the Annunciation, Mary said yes to the angel's invitation to be the bearer of God. Mary's *yes* was not a passive, submissive acceptance of her situation. Hers was a bold and faithful *yes!*

Mary said yes to a child out of wedlock. Mary said yes to fleeing her country with Joseph in order to keep that child safe. Mary said "yes, you can do this" to Jesus at the wedding at Cana. Mary said yes to standing with Jesus at the foot of the cross as he suffered and died. This was not passive acceptance. Mary's *yes* was an enthusiastic, fearless, hopeful and determined *yes* to the will of God. Her *yes* to Jesus said, "I believe in you, I have faith in you, I will not abandon you, and I will not leave you to suffer alone."

In her beautiful prayer the Magnificat, Mary proclaims, "My soul magnifies the Lord, and my spirit rejoices in God my Savior" (Luke 1:46–47). Our own call to discipleship is a call to say a bold and faithful *yes*—to magnify the Lord with our lives and to enlarge God's love in the world. This is the *yes* that we are called to proclaim even when we are faced with indecision, adversity, questions about our future and concerns about the world. Like Mary, we are called to respond with selfless love and absolute trust in God.

Finally, Mary points the way toward Jesus—the one true voice. The first chapter of John's Gospel introduces Jesus as the living Word of God. "In the beginning was the Word, and the Word was with God, and the Word was God. And the Word became flesh and lived among us" (John 1:1, 14). Jesus is the incarnate voice of God that teaches, heals and forgives. He expresses words of friendship, prayer, forgiveness and love. He says, "Follow me. Do not be afraid. Love one another." His words are the ones we are meant to hear and called to proclaim.

We need more voices like Dorothy Day and Thea Bowman—women who were able to prayerfully listen to the Spirit while actively responding to the needs of the world. We need more voices like Mary, who responded with a bold and faithful *yes* to the will of God. In a world hungry for forgiveness, compassion, and love, we need voices that are in touch with Jesus, the one true voice. The world needs *your* voice— women who listen for the Spirit that echoes deep within. Listen for that voice. Follow that voice. Find your voice and let it speak.

Chapter One

1. Rainer Maria Rilke, *Letters to a Young Poet* (New York: W.W. Norton, 1934), p. 35.
2. Neil Howe and William Strauss, *Millennials Rising: The Next Great Generation* (New York: Vintage, 2000), p. 4.
3. Sue Monk Kidd, *When the Heart Waits* (San Francisco: Harper Collins, 1990), p. 26.
4. American Bar Association, *Enrollment and Degrees Awarded 1963-2008*, available at: www.abanet.org/legaled/statistics/charts/stats%20-%201.pdf. American Association of Medical Colleges, *Table 1: Medical Students Selected Years 1965-2008*, available at: www.aamc.org/members/wim/statistics/stats08/table01.pdf. Association of Theological Schools, *2008-2009 Annual Data Tables*, available at: www.ats.edu/Resources/Publications/Documents/AnnualDataTables/2008-09AnnualDataTables.pdf
5. Elizabeth Dreyer, *Making Sense of God: A Woman's Perspective* (Cincinnati: St. Anthony Messenger Press, 2008), p. xv.
6. F. Scott Spencer. "You Just Don't Understand (or Do You?)" *A Feminist Companion to John*. Amy-Jill Levine, ed. (Cleveland: Pilgrim, 2003), p. 35.

Chapter Two

1. Ted Loder, *Guerillas of Grace* (Minneapolis: Augsburg Fortress, 1981), p. 75.
2. Robert F. Morneau, *Paths to Prayer* (Cincinnati: St. Anthony Messenger Press, 1989), p. 3.
3. Henri Nouwen, *Clowning in Rome: Reflections on Solitude, Celibacy,*

Prayer, and Contemplation (Garden City, N.Y.: Image, 1979), p. 70.

Chapter Three

1. Thomas Merton, *Thoughts in Solitude* (New York: Farrar, Straus and Giroux, 1958), p. 79.

2. Frederick Buechner, *Wishful Thinking: A Theological ABC* (New York: Harper and Row, 1973), p. 95.

3. Francine Cardman, "Singleness and Spirituality," *Spirituality Today* 35/4 (1983), pp. 304–318.

4. David Fleming, *Draw Me Into Your Friendship: A Literal Translation and a Contemporary Reading of The Spiritual Exercises* (St. Louis: Institute of Jesuit Sources, 1996), p. 27.

Chapter Four

1. From 1988 to 2008, the median age of marriage for women has risen from 23.6 to 25.6 years and from 25.9 to 27.4 for men. See U.S. Census Bureau, Current Population Survey Reports, Families and Living Arrangements. *Table MS-2: Estimated Median Age at First Marriage, by Sex: 1890 to the Present*, available at: www.census.gov/population/socdemo/hh-fam/ ms2.xls.

2. C.S. Lewis, *The Four Loves* (New York: Harcourt Brace, 1960), p. 57.

3. Lewis, p. 65.

4. Sandra M. Schneiders, *Written That You May Believe: Encountering Jesus in the Fourth Gospel* (New York: Crossroad, 1999), p. 195.

Chapter Five

1. The opening prayer "Fall in Love" has been attributed to Pedro Arrupe, S.J. There are a variety of versions available. This is the version I pray.

2. Ronald Rolheiser, *The Holy Longing: The Search for a Christian Spirituality* (New York: Doubleday, 1999), p. 198.

3. James Martin, S.J., *My Life with the Saints* (Chicago: Loyola, 2006), p. 203.

4. Richard G. Malloy, *Just Sex? Giving Young Adults What They Truly Want.* Available at: www.bustedhalo.com/features/just-sex/.

Chapter Six

1. Catholic Network of Volunteer Services 2005-2006 Membership Report, available at: www.cnvs.org/docs_PDF/news/20061220 MembershipSurvey.pdf.

2. Scott London, *A Way of Seeing: The Work of Robert Coles.* Available at: www.scottlondon.com/ articles/coles.html.

3. Alice Walker, *The Color Purple* (New York: Washington Square, 1982), p. 178.

4. Information from the U.S. Department of State includes both forced labor and sexual servitude. They estimate 800,000 people are trafficked across national borders, which does not include millions of individuals trafficked within their own countries. Approximately 80 percent of transnational victims are women and girls and up to 50 percent are minors. The majority of victims transported across national borders are females trafficked into commercial sexual exploitation. See U.S. Department of State, *Trafficking Persons Report 2008*, available at: www.state.gov/g/tip/rls/ tiprpt/2008/index.htm.

5. Elizabeth Kiem, *Child Sexual Exploitation in the USA: Not Just a Problem for Developing Nations* (New York: UNICEF, 2008), available at: www.unicef.org/infobycountry/usa_46464.html.

Books

Barry, William A. *A Friendship Life No Other: Experiences God's Amazing Embrace* (Chicago: Loyola, 2008).

Brackley, Dean. *The Call to Discernment in Troubled Times: New Perspectives on the Transformative Wisdom of Ignatius of Loyola* (New York: Crossroad, 2004).

Chicago Archdiocesan Women's Committee, *Voices for Peace: A Collection of Hope* (Chicago: Liturgy Training, 2004).

Chittister, Joan. *Scarred by Struggle; Transformed by Hope* (Grand Rapids: Eerdmans, 2005).

Coffey, Kathy. *God in the Moment: Making Every Day a Prayer* (Chicago: Loyola, 1999).

Coles, Scott. *The Call of Service* (New York: Houghton Mifflin, 1994).

Dreyer, Elizabeth A. *Making Sense of God: A Woman's Perspective,* (St. Anthony Messenger Press, 2008).

Gaillardetz, Richard. *Transforming Our Days: Spirituality, Community and Liturgy in a Technological Culture* (New York: Crossroad, 2000).

Genovesi, Vincent. *In Pursuit of Love: Catholic Morality and Human Sexuality* (Collegeville, Minn.: Liturgical, 1996).

Himes, Michael J. *Doing the Truth in Love: Conversations About God, Relationships, and Service* (Mahwah, N.J.: Paulist, 1995).

Kidd, Sue Monk. *When the Heart Waits* (San Francisco: Harper Collins, 1990).

Langford, Jeremy. *God Moments: Why Faith Really Matters to a New Generation* (Chicago: Loyola, 2001).

Miller, Richard W. *Women and the Shaping of Catholicism: Women Through the Ages* (Liguori, Mo.: Liguori, 2009).

Morneau, Robert F. *Spiritual Direction: A Path to Spiritual Maturity* (New York: Crossroad, 1992).

———. *Paths to Prayer* (Cincinnati: St. Anthony Messenger Press, 1998).

Mueller, Joan. *Living a Spirituality of Action: A Woman's Perspective.* (Cincinnati: St. Anthony Messenger Press, 2008).

O'Connor, Kathleen M. *Lamentations and the Tears of the World* (New York: Orbis, 2002).

Palmer, Parker. *Let Your Life Speak* (San Francisco: Jossey-Bass, 2000).

Paulsell, Stephanie. *Honoring the Body: Meditations on a Christian Practice* (San Francisco: Jossey-Bass, 2003).

Ross, Susan A. *For the Beauty of the Earth: Women, Sacramentality, and Justice.* Madeleva Lecture, 2006.

Rupp, Joyce. *Out of the Ordinary: Prayers, Poems, and Reflections for Every Season* (Notre Dame, Ind.: Ave Maria, 2000).

Schneiders, Sandra M. *Written That You May Believe: Encountering Jesus in the Fourth Gospel* (New York: Crossroad, 1993).

Timmerman, Joan. *Sexuality and Spiritual Growth* (New York: Crossroad, 1992). This book is out of print but worth a visit to a library, second-hand bookstore or Web site.

Wagner, Clare. *Awakening to Prayer: A Woman's Perspective* (Cincinnati: St. Anthony Messenger Press, 2009).

Weddell, Sherry. *The Catholic Spiritual Gifts Inventory* (Colorado Springs, Colo.: The Catherine of Siena Institute, 1995).

Whitehead. Evelyn Eaton, and James D. Whitehead. *A Sense of Sexuality: Christian Love and Intimacy* (New York: Doubleday, 1989).

Web Resources
Amate House: www.amatehouse.org

Busted Halo: A Web site for spiritual seekers: www.bustedhalo.com

Catholic Network of Volunteer Services: www.cnvs.org

Jesuit Volunteer Corp: www.jesuitvolunteers.org

Pray As You Go: Daily Prayer for Your MP3 Player: www.pray-as-you-go.org

Sacred Space: A 10-minute Guided Meditation based on Scripture: www.sacredspace.ie

St. Louis University's Liturgy Web site includes a variety of Scripture reflections, prayers and discussion questions based on the Sunday readings: www.liturgy.slu.edu

INDEX

Called to Holiness Series

A groundbreaking eight-volume series on women's spirituality, *Called to Holiness: Spirituality for Catholic Women* will cover the many diverse facets of a woman's interior life and help her discover how God works with her and through her. An ideal resource for a woman seeking to find how God charges the moments of her life—from spirituality itself, to the spirituality of social justice, the spirituality of grieving the loss of a loved one, the creation and nurturing of families, the mentoring of young adult Catholic women, to recognition of the shared wisdom of women in the middle years—this series can be used by individuals or in groups. Far from the cloister or monastery, these books find God in the midst of a woman's everyday life and help her to find and celebrate God's presence day to day and acknowledge her own gifts as an ordinary "theologian." The books can be used independently or together for individual discussion or group faith sharing. Each book will include gathering rituals, reflection questions and annotated bibliographies.

Making Sense of God
A Woman's Perspective
Elizabeth A. Dreyer

The moment is ripe for ordinary Catholic women to "do Christian theology." Times such as these challenge us to be holy, to be alive in the Spirit, to summon the energy and make the commitment to help one another grow spiritually. Now is the time for Catholic women to make sense of God.

In this introductory volume to the *Called to Holiness* series, Catholic theologian Elizabeth Dreyer encourages us to acknowledge our dignity, harvest our gifts and empower all women in church and society. Dreyer helps us to shape what we think about God, justice, love, prayer, family life, the destiny of humanity and the entire universe.

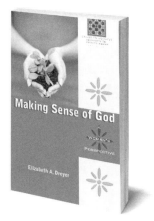

Paper, 128 pp.
Order #B16884
ISBN 978-0-86716-884-6
$11.95

Living a Spirituality of Action
A Woman's Perspective
Joan Mueller

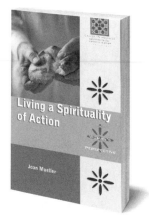

"Own your gifts and use them to make the world a better place," Catholic theologian Joan Mueller writes. In this practical book she provides us with ideas and encouragement to live and act with courage to change the world, even if our actions are sometimes small.

This is a book for all who hear about hungry people living in the park and decide to make sandwiches, who volunteer to teach children to read, who raise money to change systems that provide substandard care to the vulnerable, who can imagine a mothered world. Mueller invites us to discuss and embrace our shared wisdom.

Paper, 112 pp.
Order #B16885
ISBN 978-0-86716-885-3
$11.95

Grieving With Grace
A Woman's Perspective
Dolores R. Leckey

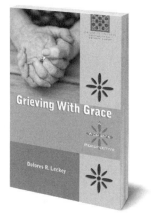

There are many ways in which the course of our daily lives can be altered—illness, change in residence, loss of employment and death of loved one. These alterations can require dramatic and even subtle changes in our everyday living, limit our options and force us to choose different priorities.

Dolores Leckey knows firsthand that the death of a spouse changes forever the rhythms of life at all levels—body, mind and soul. In this moving and personal narrative that includes entries from her journal, she shares with us her own shift in consciousness, in the way she sees God, herself and the world after her husband's death. She offers us consolation and hope.

Paper, 112 pp.
Order #B16888
ISBN 978-0-86716-888-4
$11.95

Awakening to Prayer
A Woman's Perspective
Clare Wagner

The word "prayer" is almost as generic as *food* or *book*, says Clare Wagner in *Awakening to Prayer: A Woman's Perspective,* and the varieties of prayer forms are countless. In this best and worst of times, Wagner writes, it is intriguing to ponder how women of the twenty-first century pray and enter into a relationship with Holy Presence.

To help us see anew, she draws on the wisdom of the Scriptures, the insights of the mystics and the experience of ordinary, vibrant women and men living in our midst. She offers suggestions of words to use and rituals to experience to help us awaken to prayer.

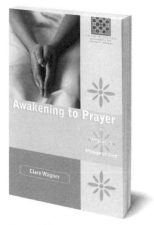

Paper, 112 pp.
Order #B16892
ISBN 978-0-86716-892-1
$11.95

Embracing Latina Spirituality
A Woman's Perspective
Michelle A. Gonzalez

Latinas treat the sacred in ways that are similar to the ways we treat those we encounter every day: They converse with statues of saints and Mary, leave them flowers and light candles to persuade them to gain favor for us, and become angry when prayers are not answered. These everyday aspects of Latina spirituality reflect a strong sense of family and community that we can embrace as a refreshing spiritual alternative to the individualism that permeates our society.

Entering into the world of Latina spirituality offers new ways to understand self and community and to approach prayer, diversity and the struggle against oppression. Latina spirituality provides us an entry point into true unity.

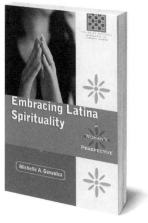

Paper, 112 pp.
Order #B16886
ISBN 978-0-86716-886-0
$11.95

Creating New Life, Nurturing Families
A Woman's Perspective
Sidney Callahan

What makes a woman a hero? Does she need to possess almost super-human qualities? Must she grab headlines or set out to save our world? No, says Sidney Callahan. A hero is simply a woman who makes small, daily self-sacrifices out of love for others. Nowhere is this definition more embodied than in the love of wives and mothers for their families.

Digging deeply into the various dimensions of women's journeys and discussing love and marriage, sex, mothering, work and transforming joy amidst suffering, Callahan shows how a woman's commitment to the well-being of her husband and children is a participation in the very life of the Trinity. She explores the many ways that a wife and mother pours out her love for her family, as Christ poured out his love for us, and shows how that humbling of yourself, day after day, ensures that God's message of hope and salvation will be passed on to generations to come.

Paper, 144 pp.
Order #B16893
ISBN 978-0-86716-893-8
$11.95

ABOUT THE AUTHOR

BETH M. KNOBBE, a campus minister at the Sheil Catholic Center of Northwestern University, graduated in 2007 with a master's degree in divinity from the Catholic Theological Union in Chicago. As a campus minister, she mentors students and organizes retreats and service trips. A member of the Catholic Campus Ministry Association, she speaks often about young adult spirituality. She has had articles published in *U.S. Catholic* and *The Word on Campus*.